THE LOUVRE MURDER CLUB

Editing: Christine Schultz-Touge

www.lepassage-editions.fr

CHRISTOS MARKOGIANNAKIS

THE LOUVRE MURDER CLUB

A CRIMINARTISTIC TOUR WITHIN THE LOUVRE

LEPASSAGE

No one has ever written, painted, sculpted, modeled, built, or invented except literally to get out of hell.

Antonin Artaud
Van Gogh, the Man Suicided by Society

SUMMARY

INTRODUCTION 8

CRIMES AND PUNISHMENTS 13
PENAL CODE · DIVINE JUSTICE · LEX TALIONIS

MOMMY DEAREST 19
GIGANTICIDE

THE STIGMATIZED MURDERESSES 23
WOMEN WHO KILL · STIGMATIZATION

THE SON'S RETURN 29
CONSPIRATORS · CRIMINAL BEHAVIOUR FACTORS · MATRICIDE

NO OTHER KING, UNDER MY REIGN 35
MASS MURDER · CHILD MURDER

THE UNWANTED REWARD 41
ABETTOR · FEMME FATALE

IN THE NAME OF THE FATHER, THE SON, AND THE HOLY ROOSTER 47
BLASPHEMY · REGICIDE

ONE WAY OR ANOTHER 53
DUEL · SINGLE COMBAT

A RECURRING NIGHTMARE 61
POLITICAL MASSACRE · PROSCRIPTIONS

OUR ANCESTOR, THE FIRST MURDERER 69
FRATRICIDE · PHYSIOGNOMIC THEORIES

A FAMILY VENDETTA 75
VENDETTA · MASSACRE

A MOTHER'S REVENGE 81
WOMEN WHO KILL · REVENGE KILLING

THE SLAYING OF BEAUTY 87
MEANS · MOTIVE · OPPORTUNITY

THE SEDUCER WITH THE SWORD 93
WOMEN WHO KILL · HEROIC MURDERESS

A HUNDRED EYES FOREVER SHUT 99
TERATOCIDE

THE STATE ABOVE FAMILY 105
CAPITAL SENTENCE

THE INVISIBLE MURDERESS 113
ASSASSINATION · WOMEN WHO KILL · CRIME SCENE

THE EVERLASTING HUNT 121
JUSTICE · PHYSIOGNOMIC SIGNS · NATURAL-BORN KILLER

SON AND HUSBAND. FATHER AND BROTHER. DETECTIVE AND MURDERER 127
DETECTIVE FICTION · REGICIDE · PATRICIDE

THINKING TWICE 135
MARITICIDE · WOMEN WHO KILL

BETTER DEAD THAN SURRENDERED 143
DEMOCIDE · CRIMINAL LABELLING THEORY

THE DAUGHTER'S HONOUR 155
PREMEDITATED MURDER · CRIME OF PASSION · FILICIDE · HONOUR KILLING

THE KING IS MURDERED, LONG LIVE THE MURDERER 163
REGICIDE · DNA TESTING

SACRED NIGHT, BLOODY NIGHT 169
MASSACRE · GENOCIDE

ANTIQUITY'S DEXTER MORGAN 177
SERIAL KILLER

YOUTH UNDER PERSECUTION 183
PERSECUTION

SEARCHING FOR THE TRUTH 189
INFANTICIDE · PEDICIDE · CRIMINOLOGICAL THEORY OF SOCIAL REACTION

EPILOGUE 197

SELECTIVE BIBLIOGRAPHY 200

INTRODUCTION

"A society free of crime is quite impossible" according to the 19th-century French sociologist Emile Durkheim.[1] Crime is an omnipresent and "normal" condition in every civilization, at any time, anywhere.

And as with most activities within any group, crime has been represented in art over time. But not all crime is worth depicting. Artists have always been inspired, not by petty crimes, but by the most sensational ones, those that trigger intense feelings in their spectators and readers. Murder is a great example of this.

In descriptive arts, nine out of ten dramas, comedies or novels contain one or more crimes. On the contrary, in the visual arts, only one out of ten paintings – and even less sculptures – represent crime as a main or secondary subject.[2]

There is no better place to see these representations than at the Louvre, the most frequented museum in the world, housing the work of civilizations from Antiquity up to the

1. Emile Durkheim, *Les Règles de la méthode sociologique* (1894), Paris: P.U.F., 1960, pp. 65–72.

2. Enrico Ferri, *Les Criminels dans l'art et la littérature* (1908).

mid-19th century. Throughout its long aisles and halls, murder is present by canvas, marble, wood and clay.

Visitors can bear witness to all kinds of killings: historical, factual or fictitious, premeditated, in cold blood or in high passion. These murders might be the outcome of revenge or justice, committed in times of trouble, war or peace; they might be massacres or duels. Among the scenery and the eras, victims and perpetrators vary too; they can be men, women, gods or monsters.

In a museum, De Quincey's theory on murder as one of the fine arts can be more palpably acknowledged: We do not need to grasp murder by its moral or punitive handle; this would make no sense at all. What is done is done, we are not here to prevent or judge the deed; we stand before a work of art – before a crime scene – in order to enjoy it.

Thus the act of killing presented in art is nothing but an aesthetic experience, a sublime one at that.[1] As a visitor to the Louvre, you stand as an eyewitness to the murder scene, present yet detached from the perpetrator and the victim, vulnerable yet immune to them. You, contrary to the victim, experience terror at a distance, without the lurid torment of suspense, and unlike the assailant, you face no potential punishment.[2] Unlike the victim you are safe from a physical point of view. Unlike the killer, you face no moral agony.[3] Thus you encounter murder as a sublimated and purely aesthetic trigger.

1. Thomas De Quincey, "On Murder Considered as One of the Fine Arts," *Blackwood's Magazine*, (1827).
2. Joel Black, *The aesthetics of Murder*, The John Hopkins University Press, 1991.
3. As in 2.

This aesthetic perspective of murder is the inspiration and the epicentre of *Criminart*, a movement connecting these two elements (crime and art) in theory and practice. From this perspective – the Criminartistic one – we'll explore some of the key works of art of this genre in the Louvre. We'll discover the crime scenes, the motives of the represented personages or the artists, the truths and the lies behind each murder. We'll learn the stories of victims and assailants and uncover the symbolism and the artistic keys of expression, which lie under the surface.

The art interpreted in this book is not restricted to the legal – sensu stricto – definition of murder,[1] or even by the term homicide.[2] Here we will see works depicting the *taking of one's life by someone else*. The victim or the perpetrator might be human or not; the killing might be the fruit of revenge, punishment or cold-blooded murder.

Furthermore, the examples that follow are not exhaustive. The choice of the works is based on a personal selection of favourites, from various eras and cultures, many types of crime, and of course different forms of art (from painting to sculpture, from decorative to functional objects).

This Criminartistic tour within the Louvre is presented in chronological order, starting from 2nd-millennium BC Mesopotamia up to 19th-century France.

Before we embark upon this Criminartistic adventure, keep in mind that every museum, as a vessel of life-representations is alive too. Like every living organism it moves, changes,

1. The unlawful killing of a human being with malice aforethought.

2. The killing of one human being by another human being.

evolves. So don't be surprised if some of the artworks in this book may not be exhibited where you expect them. They may be in restoration or loaned out to other exhibitions, or quite simply have been moved to another part of the Louvre.

But no matter where they are, their truth remains the same. And this truth we will uncover.

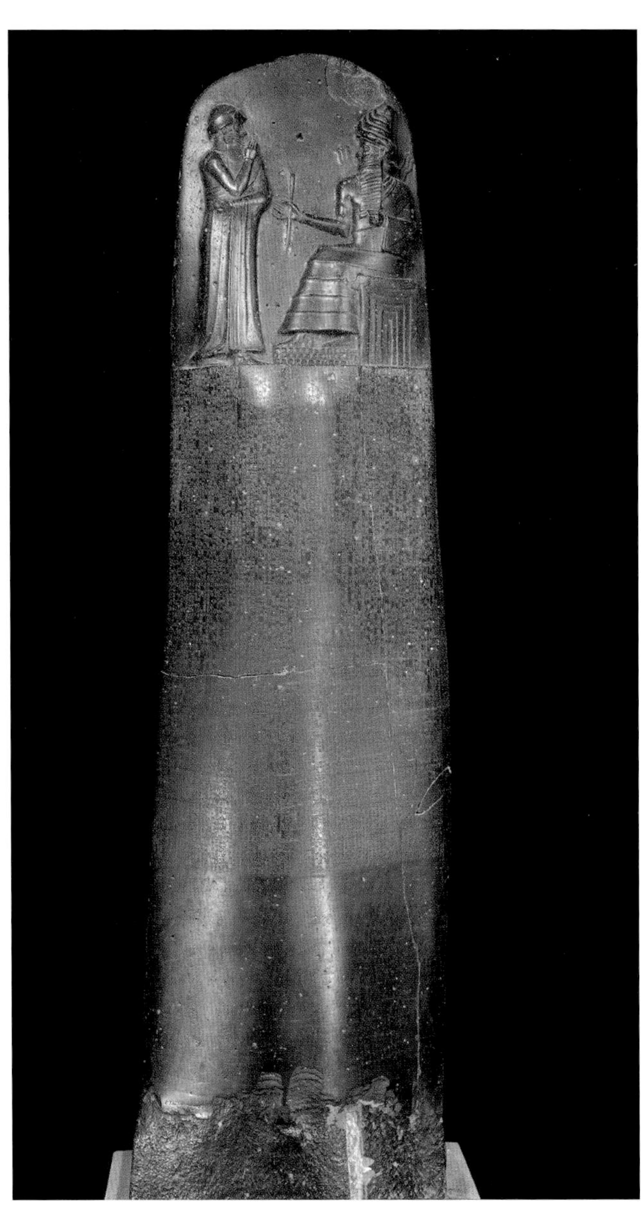

CHAPTER 1
CRIMES AND PUNISHMENTS

PENAL CODE · DIVINE JUSTICE · LEX TALIONIS

The Code of Hammurabi, Babylonian King
1792–1750 BC
Basalt. H: 225 cm

Ground Floor, Richelieu,
Mesopotamia–2nd millennium BC, Room 3

Before we dive into our murderous adventures among perpetrators and victims, this first exhibit offers a glimpse of the consequences that follow crime. As we shall see in many of the art works, crime and punishment go together, no matter if the latter is an act of human revenge, divine wrath or State power.

A Law Code is a systematized collection of regulations, rules, or statutes of a particular jurisdiction.[1] More specifically a Criminal or Penal code is the aggregate of statutory enactments pertaining to criminal offenses, a systematic and integrated statement of the rules and principles pertaining to criminal offenses.[2]

The stele before us is one of the world's oldest known regulations codes. The laws were inscribed on basalt stone by the 18th-century BC Babylonian[3] King Hammurabi. It was discovered in 1901 by a team of French archaeologists in the ancient city of Susa, in what is now known as Iran. It consists of 282 laws regulating, amongst others things, family relations

---

1. *Webster's New World Law Dictionary*, Jonathan Wallace, Susan Ellis Wild, Wiley Publishing Inc, 2006, p. 76.
2. http://dictionary.reference.com
3. Babylon was an important city in ancient Mesopotamia, situated between the Tigris and Euphrates rivers.

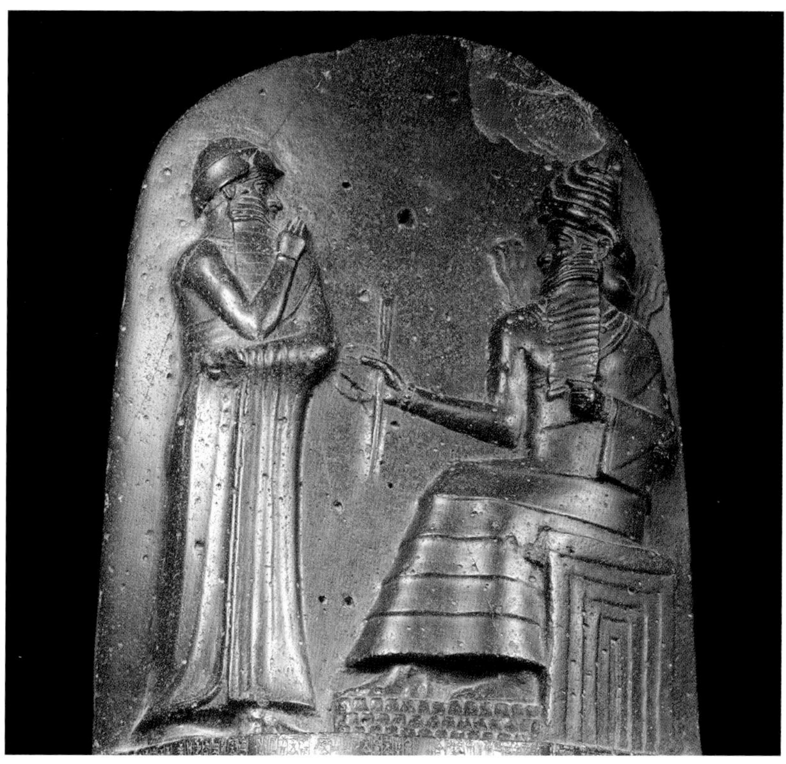

and civil conduct, trade, slavery, contracts, duties of workers and criminal offences.

Hammurabi by his own description is the "wisest, bravest and most fierce, sublime and most mighty, most gifted, most righteous and just of men". Thus he is the chosen one, selected by the gods who appointed him to establish the laws for his empire in ancient Mesopotamia. On the highest point of the stele we see the king facing Shamash, the Mesopotamian Sun god. Shamash was also considered the god of justice, bringing light to criminal matters, in the same way the sun dissolves darkness. We see him seated on a throne (note how he would dwarf the mortal king if he were to stand) beams of light rising from his shoulders. He hands over the symbols of authority, a rod and a ring, to Hammurabi. The sceptre looks like a chisel with which the god-favoured king – humbled by the god's presence and hiding his face with his hand – will enshrine the laws in stone.

Thus, the text under the depiction is dictated by divine justice. The applied penalties for crimes against property, physical integrity and life vary according to the social class and gender of the victim and/or the perpetrator.

Its main characteristic can be found in this aphorism: "an eye for an eye, a tooth for a tooth". This is the foundation of the *lex talionis*, a form of retaliatory justice, and serves as the basis for Hammurabi's code. "If a man destroys the eye of another man, they shall destroy his own eye. If one breaks a man's bone, they shall break his own bone."

In the same spirit, sentences are severe even for matters that nowadays would appear of minor importance, with many transgressions punished by death. Thus capital punishment is applied to "whoever falsely accuses someone of a capital crime", "steals the property or receives stolen goods of a temple or the city", "steals gold or silver", "or steals the underage son of another". The death sentence was also applied to robbers or to the "builder of a house that collapses and kills the owner". Furthermore, if by the collapse it is the family's son who is killed, "the capital sentence is applied to the builder's son". If someone broke into a house by digging a hole in the wall, he was killed and buried in front of this hole. Death by drowning was applied to the "wife that neglected her husband, left him and ruined their household". The same sentence was applied to the "father who had intercourse with the woman he betrothed to his son". Death by burning was the punishment for "incest between mother and son".

While legislation normally evolves with social changes, Hammurabi wanted his laws to remain intact, for eternity. The lowest part of the stele serves as a clear warning to whomever tries to change his "valuable, wise and righteous words".

The Prince who disrespects gods and defies the laws written by the wisest of men shall face his curse and contempt. The misfortunes that will fall upon the ruler who defaces Hammurabi's laws, falsifies his words, changes his memorial, or extinguishes his name and writes down his own name are unforgiving. Amongst others, his sceptre will be broken, his life shortened, insurrection will be uncontrollable, his country and people will be destroyed, his troops exterminated rendering him powerless to surrender to his enemy. Water will disappear, day will turn into night, sickness and wounds will prevail that no physician will understand or be able to cure.

Curses, threats, spells and warnings aside, Hammurabi – the "Sun of Babylon" no matter how strong, clever, tireless, valiant, irresistible as the fighter he described himself to be – faced the same fate as so many rulers before and after him: He was outdated by reality.

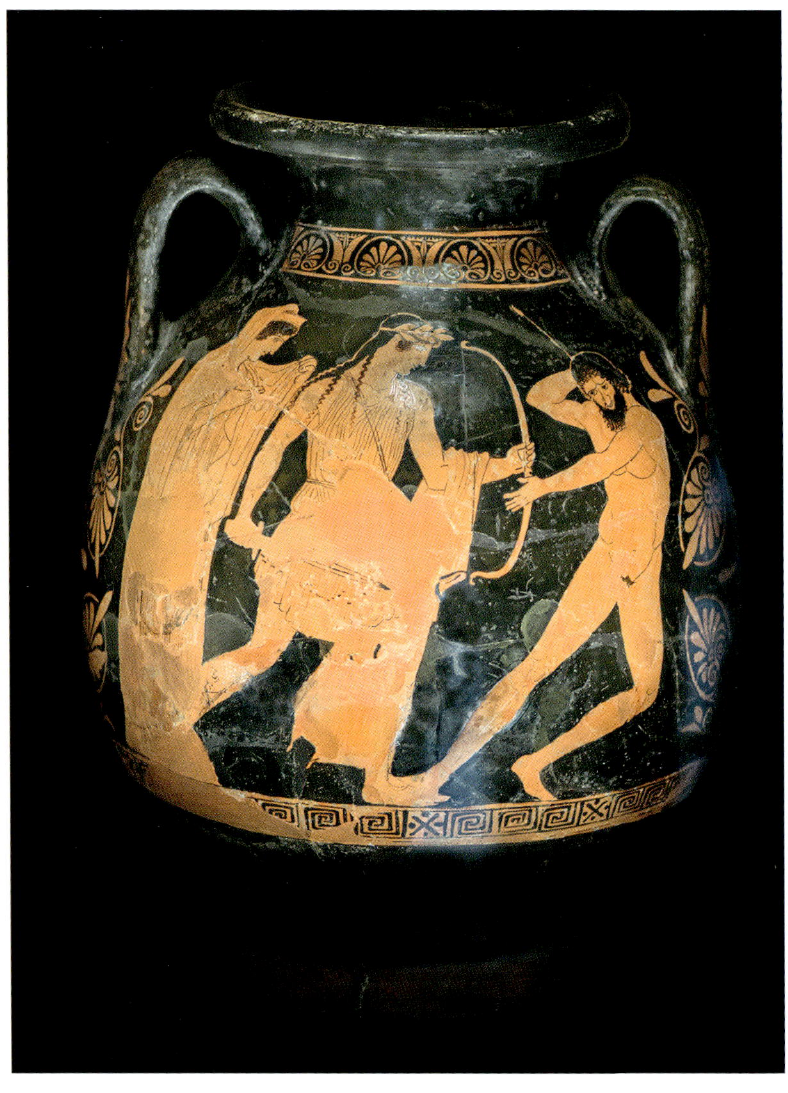

CHAPTER 2
MOMMY DEAREST

GIGANTICIDE

Polygnotos, *Apollo Killing Tityus in the Presence of Leto*
Athens, about 450–440 BC
Pelike with red figures, H: 44.5 cm; D: 34.5 cm

First Floor, Sully, Campana Gallery IV, Room 43, Display case 12

Ancient Greek gods were far from perfect. They had the same qualities and vices as mortals which, when combined with limitless power, proved to be dangerous for their adversaries.

Apollo was no exception. He was the god of light, arts and prophecy. Yet, despite his artistic and luminous nature, he could prove to be excessively cruel, especially where his mother Leto and her honour were concerned.

Leto was one of Zeus' many mistresses. When she became pregnant with his children, his wife Hera[1] was enraged and initiated her revenge. Leto would not be permitted to give birth on any land under the sun. Furthermore, no man was to accommodate her for fear of Hera's wrath. After wandering and being rejected in every place on earth, Leto was finally accepted on a small island in the Aegean Sea, called Delos. There, after nine days and nights of agonizing pain Artemis[2] and her twin brother Apollo were born. He was to become the god of the Sun and Arts, and she was the goddess of the Moon and Hunting.

It's little wonder Leto's children were protective of their mother. In addition to the Massacre of the Niobids (see chapter

1. A.k.a. Junon in Roman mythology.
2. A.k.a. Diana in Roman mythology.

"A Family Vendetta") the scene playing out on this black and red vase is yet another testimony of that protective love.

When Leto travelled to Delphi from Phocis, a Giant[1] named Tityus, also a son of Zeus, fell in love with her. When she resisted his approaches, he grabbed her with his massive hands and attempted to rape her. At that instant Apollo and his sister came to the rescue of their mother and killed Tityus.

The scene on the vase depicts the exact moment of the Giganticide, meaning the act of killing a giant. Having already shot Tityus with his arrows, Apollo is about to finish him off with his sword. Behind him his mother hides her face with her cloak, not willing to witness the slaying taking place before her.

Yet death was not the giant's final punishment. In the underworld, Tityus would be tied and stretched for eternity to a length of nine plethrons (a plethron is an ancient Greek measurement unit that equals approximately 30 metres) with two vultures feasting on his liver, day and night.

As we shall see again, one should stay away from the gods in this museum. Being their opponent, or even their favoured one, could mean nothing but trouble.

---

1. In Greek mythology, the Giants or Gigantes were a strong and aggressive, usually huge in shape, race.

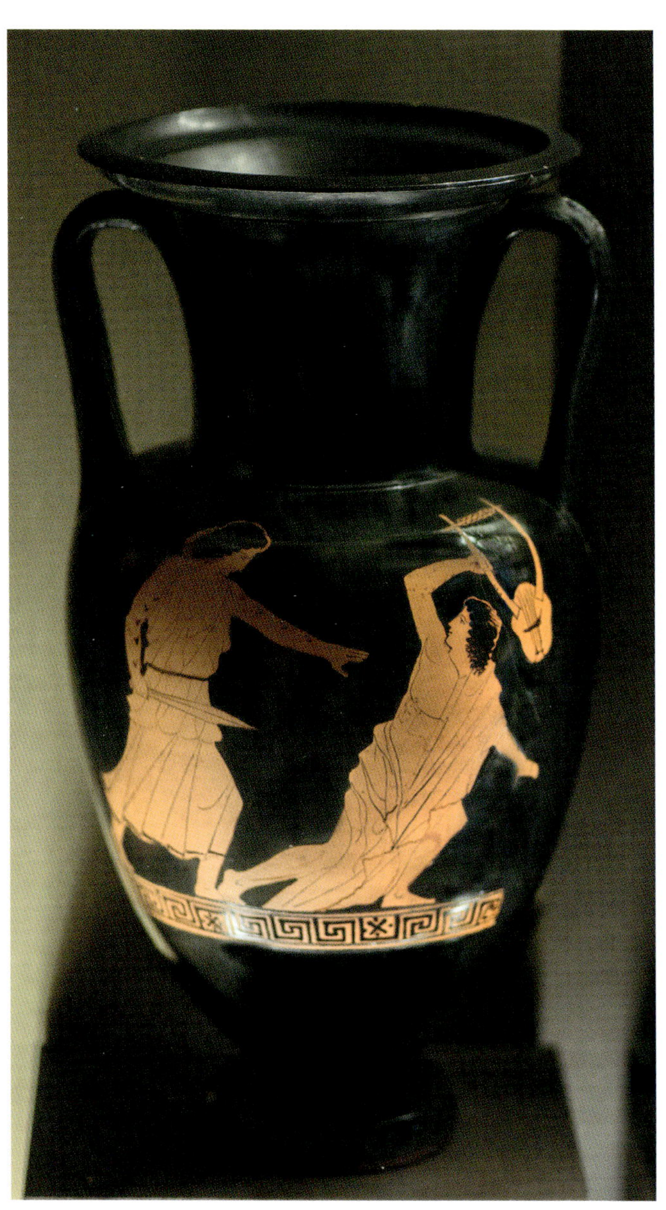

CHAPTER 3
THE STIGMATIZED MURDERESSES

WOMEN WHO KILL - STIGMATIZATION

Orpheus' Death, Athens, about 445–440 BC
Amphora with red figures, H: 32.9 cm; D: 17.4 cm

First Floor, Sully, Campana Gallery IV, Room 43, Display case 13

Orpheus was the most talented and renowned poet and singer in ancient Greece. He was the son of Calliope, the Muse of Poetry, and Oeagrus, a Thracian[1] king. Orpheus played the lyre (a harp-like instrument) that was given to him by Apollo, the god of Music. His songs spoke of love and universal truths and even foretold the future. His music was so beautiful that it was said to charm not only humans and animals but also rocks and plants. Myth has it that his notes could even change the flow of rivers. Yet his great talent in music and prophecies could not protect him from the unfortunate events that would come to pass throughout his lifetime. Nor did it prevent his violent death.

The myth of Orpheus and his wife Eurydice is well known. On the day of their wedding, Eurydice was bitten by a viper and died. When Orpheus discovered her body, his sorrow was expressed through music on his lyre. The songs were so sad that even the gods wept. So on their advice, Orpheus descended to the underworld. There with his music he softened the heart of Hades, the god of Death, who allowed Eurydice to return to Earth on one condition: that her husband walk ahead of her and not look back until they both had reached the

1. Thrace was then and still is in the northern part of Greece.

upper world. His longing to see his wife again was such that, as soon as Orpheus stepped into the upper world he turned to look at her. But Eurydice was still a few steps behind… in the underworld. And at that instant she vanished again, this time for good.

The scene on the amphora vase takes place after this sad event. It shows the young poet's murder: an angry woman, is about to fatally penetrate him with her sword.

With his wife dead forever, Orpheus started wandering alone in the Thracian forests. He never looked at another woman again and his only companions were his musical notes and Thracian men who, enchanted by his music, followed him. Orpheus withheld his music and prophecies from the Thracian women. He would not allow any of them near him, as they served as a painful reminder of his wife. Because his songs were no longer lavishing praise on female beauty and grace, the Thracian men, hypnotized by the sad tunes, fell into each other's arms.

Their rejected wives became mad with jealous rage and decided to kill Orpheus. Yet the sticks and stones they threw at him were charmed by his melodies and refused to strike him. So the women seized their swords.

This is the scene we witness on the amphora vase. It is the moment that a Thracian woman is about to kill the poet, decapitate him and then cut him into pieces. He attempts to use his lyre as a shield, but to no avail.[1] His head and musical instrument will be thrown unceremoniously into the Evros[2]

1. Exh. cat. *L'épopée des rois thraces*, Musée du Louvre, Somogy, 2015.

2. A river that runs in the interior of the modern days Balkans.

River. His scull is said to have continued singing all along the way to Lesbos Island,[1] where the locals recuperated it and built a temple in Orpheus' honour. The Muses[2] picked up his Lyre and delivered it to the heavens where it became a constellation known as Lyra.

Meanwhile back in Thrace, his male disciples were determined that this crime would not go unpunished. They ensured that everyone would know that their women were murderesses at first sight. They tattooed the women's arms with black V-shaped marks (you can see these along the woman's arms on this vase).

This kind of tattoo – known as stigma in Greek (*στίγμα*) – was a means of communicating that someone was a criminal. And from this practice came the word stigmatize, which literally means "to set some mark of disgrace or infamy upon someone".

1. Greek island located in the north-eastern Aegean Sea.
2. The Muses in Greek mythology were goddesses of artistic and scientific inspiration.

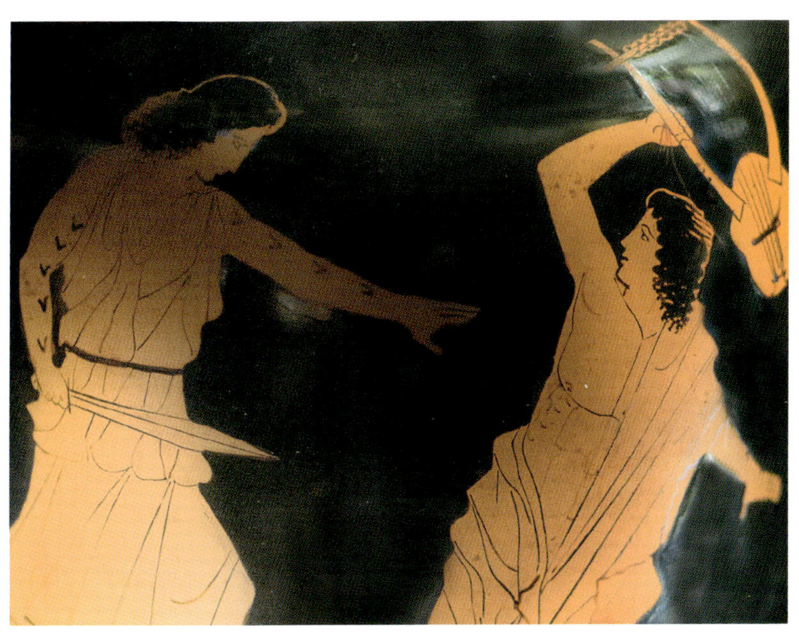

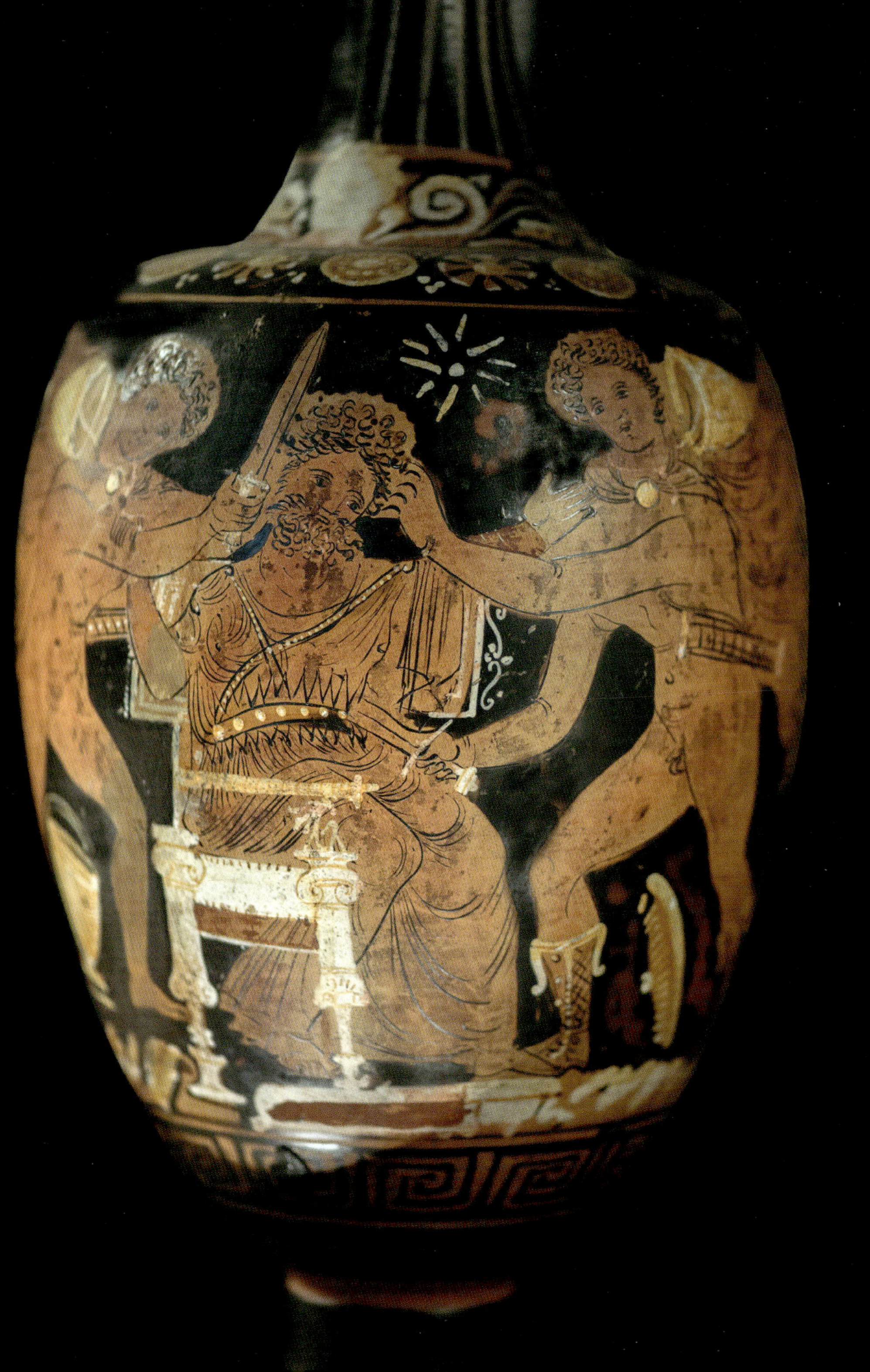

CHAPTER 4
THE SON'S RETURN

CONSPIRATORS · CRIMINAL BEHAVIOUR FACTORS · MATRICIDE

Orestes and Pylades Killing Aegisthus, Apulia, about 320–300 BC
Oenochoe with red figures, H: 49 cm; D: 17.4 cm

First Floor, Sully, Campana Gallery,
Room 39, Display case 7 (Tragic Themes)

In every legal case, especially when murder is involved, there are always two sides to be considered. Sympathies vary with either side, depending on the perceptions of the witnesses, or of each member of the jury. This is the reality in normal life, where gods, destiny and cursed families have no place. Suffice to say, in Greek mythology, things are different.

In the red figure vase before us we see Orestes and his cousin Pylades, attacking Aegisthus. The two cousins are conspirators, as two or more people who agree to commit a crime are called.[1] Yet, all three men we see here are bound by family ties. The respective family history is a landscape splattered with spilt blood and betrayal.

Orestes' paternal grandfather, Atreus, and Aegisthus' father Thyestes were brothers. The two had agreed to reign over the kingdom of Mycenae alternately. But when his time was up, Atreus did not hand over to Thyestes the golden sheepskin – the symbol of royal power – and continued to rule alone.

Thyestes stole the golden sheepskin and took power. Still, Thyestes promised his brother Atreus to give him back the throne if ever the sun was to rise from the west. And with Zeus' help, it did. Atreus took back the kingdom once again and exiled his brother.

1. https://www.law.cornell.edu/wex/conspiracy

But the score was yet to be settled. After some time, Atreus recalled his brother Thyestes to the kingdom under the pretence of forgiveness. At the reconciliation table, a very special meal was served. Atreus had killed the sons of Thyestes, cooked them up and offered them as a meal to their father. When the dead boys' heads were revealed, Thyestes full of grief and fury put a curse on Atreus and started planning his own revenge.

Thyestes asked for the gods' help, and it came in the form of a prophecy: if he had a son with his own daughter, this son would kill Atreus. And so it came to pass. The son, named Aegisthus, whom Thyestes had with his own daughter, would indeed kill Atreus. But blood calls for more blood. When Atreus' son, the new Mycenae king, Agamemnon, left for Troy, Aegisthus took Agamemnon's wife Clytemnestra as a mistress and seized the throne.

Orestes, Agamemnon's son, was just a child at the time. His sister Electra sent him, under a cloak of secrecy, to the royal court of Phokis,[1] where Agamemnon's sister was the queen. Having escaped Mycenae, Orestes' life was spared from Aegisthus who wanted to rid the kingdom of its legitimate heir. Pylades, the second standing figure on the oenochoe jug, was Phokis' royal prince. The two young men grew up together, became best friends and set off together to live the adventures and misadventures Orestes was soon to face.

When Orestes discovered that his father had been murdered and thrown to the vultures without a proper burial, he swore revenge upon the two murderers: his mother

1. Phocis was a region in the central part of ancient Greece, including Delphi.

Clytemnestra and her lover Aegisthus (see chapter "Thinking Twice"). But first he needed to get within striking range. So he returned to Mycenae under a false identity, bearing the "good news of Orestes' death". The trap was set.

This is the scene we witness. After relief and joy from the belief that – with Orestes dead – his reign and life were no longer in jeopardy, a piercing truth descends upon Aegisthus. We see him seated in Agamemnon's throne reigning over his country, living with his wife. His representation is rather feminine. Under his Oriental long dress, we can detect breasts, which in contrast to his bearded face underline the anomaly of a tyrannical despot.[1]

In a violent movement, overturning the vase between his legs, Pylades grabs Aegisthus' hair from behind and holds his sword at neck level. His cousin Orestes stabs him with his sword, just under the heart. Aegisthus will fall dead. Then it's the turn of Orestes to kill his mother, Clytemnestra, committing matricide.

On the extreme left of the vase, a menacing female figure with snakes on her head is watching the conspirators. She is one of the Erinyes[2] and she will guarantee that the murderers will be prosecuted, no matter how justified their crimes.[3] So revenge is rendered justly, but the chapter of the last male descendant in this cursed family story, is not yet closed.

---

1. *L'Ilioupersis dans la céramique italiote. Les mythes et leur expression figurée au IVᵉ siècle*, Jean-Marc Moret, Bibliotheca Helvetica Romana, XIV, 1975.
2. In Greek mythology the Furies or the Erinyes were female spirits of justice and vengeance, pursuing criminals, especially murderers and driving them mad.
3. "Iconographie et problèmes de mise en scène : La mort d'Égisthe dans les 'Choéphores' d'Eschyle", *Revue Archéologique*, 1978, Presses Universitaires de France, p. 43.

For centuries, scientists have been trying to determine the factors of criminal behaviour. Are criminal tendencies inherited? Are they written in the DNA? Or are they a result of sociological factors, especially early life experiences and/or family surroundings? These questions are still unanswered. Yet this family could serve as a case study, par excellence.

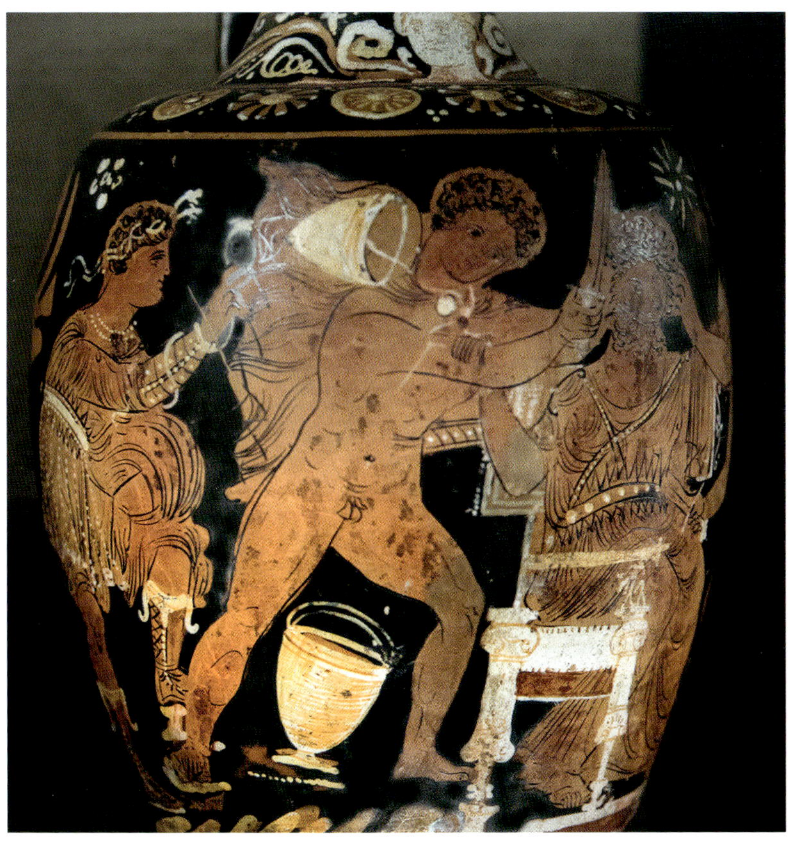

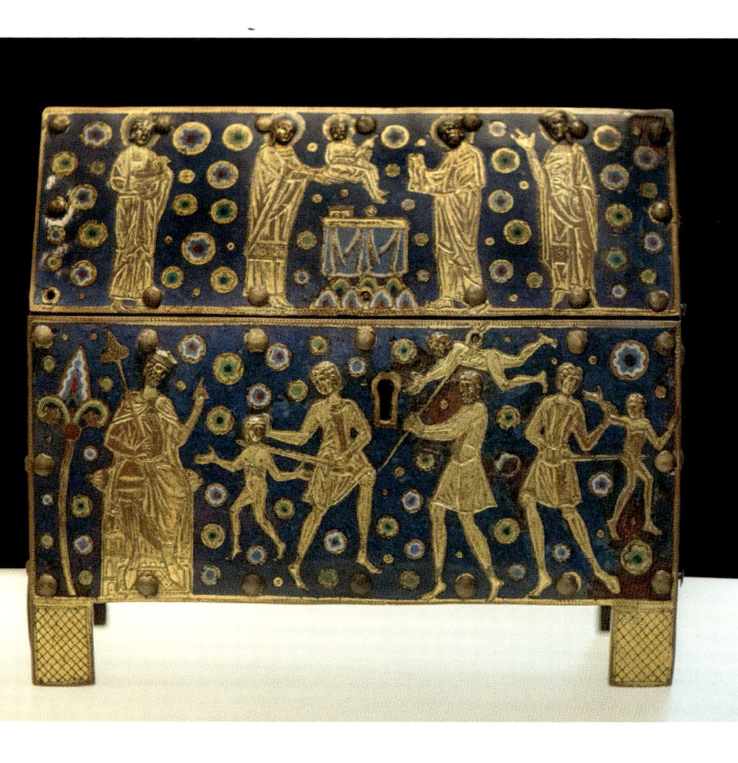

CHAPTER 5
NO OTHER KING, UNDER MY REIGN

MASS MURDER - CHILD MURDER

Anonymous, *The Massacre of the Innocents*,
Limoges, last quarter of the 12th century
Box, enamel on gilded copper. H: 18.8 cm; L: 21,7 cm; D: 9 cm

First Floor, Richelieu, Suger, Room 2, Display case 22

Mass murder, the act of murdering many people simultaneously, or over a relatively short period of time[1] is one of the most shocking forms of killing. Furthermore, child murder is one of the most appalling crimes. If these two forms of murder were to be combined the result would be horrendous.

On its lower half, the object we have before us recounts the story of an infamous children's massacre, as described in the Bible, which, along with Greek mythology, is a voluminous source of violent and murderous events.

Verses 13–16 in the second chapter of the Gospel of Matthew in the New Testament read: "When [the Magi] had gone, an angel of the Lord appeared to Joseph in a dream. Get up, he said, take the child and his mother and escape to Egypt. Stay there until I tell you, for Herod is going to search for the child to kill him. So he got up, took the child and his mother during the night and left for Egypt, where he stayed until the death of Herod. [...]

Then Herod, when he saw that he was mocked by the wise men, was exceedingly angry, and sent out, and killed all the male children, who were in Bethlehem and in all the surrounding

1. "Mass Murder" A. Aggrawal, in Payne-James J.J., Byard R.W., Corey, T.S., Henderson, C. (eds.) *Encyclopedia of Forensic and Legal Medicine*, vol. 3, London: Elsevier Academic Press, 2005, pp. 216–23.

countryside, from two years old and under, according to the exact time which he had learned from the wise men."

In this passage we read the reason behind the scenario unfolding before us: the so-called "Massacre of the Holy Innocents". On the left, King Herod is seated on his throne. His face and robe are depicted in detail, chiselled in gold,[1] his hand is in an authoritative gesture. Though not literally present, he oversees the killing of all the children of Bethlehem to avoid being dethroned by the new-born King of the Jews, whose birth had been announced to him by the wise men (the Magi of the biblical text).

The naturalistic depiction of the scene, sculptured by sensitive and finely finished engraving[2] is vivid in movement and atrocious in sight. The contrast between the three defenceless children and their executioners, armed with spear and swords, is extremely dramatic.[3] One is decapitated alive, the other two pierced by the King's soldiers. And these victims are just some of the many that were supposedly slaughtered.

This episode is questioned by many historians, who claim that the story is nothing but legend or folklore. What we do know as a fact is that Herod was notorious for his suspicious, vengeful and paranoid nature. Unpopular and feeling under constant threat, he would kill whomever he thought was a potential danger to his throne. This would include his predecessors, army and administration officials, even members of his

1. R. J. Vinson, "Émaux de Limoge", *Connaissance des arts*, no. 238, December 1971, p. 82.

2. Exh. cat. *Enamels of Limoges: 1100–1350*, Musée du Louvre, Metropolitan Museum of Art, New York, 1996, p. 168.

3. *L'Épée, Usages, mythes et symboles*, Paris Musée du Cluny, Musée National de Moyen Âge, 28 April–26 September 2011.

own family (one of his wives and three of his sons included). Many of these murders are recorded by historians, including Titus Flavius Josephus.[1]

So when a prophecy that announced the new-born King of the Jews eventually reached his ears, it's not surprising that he would invoke measures to prevent the baby from taking his throne. However, there is no mention in any historical archive or record of three thousand, fourteen thousand or sixty-four thousand babies being slaughtered under Herod, as Matthew's gospel or Byzantine and Syrian folklore respectively claim. Yet, if a massacre of this scale had occurred, we would expect it to be recorded by historians. The reason it wasn't may lie in the number of the victims.

In Herod's times, according to Josephus, Bethlehem was a city of about one thousand inhabitants. Taking into account population and historical statistics the number of male infants younger than two years old would have been between 4 and 40.[2] Thus, the tally of victims could not have amounted to the exaggerated scores of three thousand, fourteen thousand or sixty-four thousand babies.

So during the reign of a king who would kill hundreds, even thousands of his people, (many of them notable) the slaying of a couple of dozen children from a small unimportant peasant town, might not have been considered noteworthy.

But whether the slaughtered children numbered just four or tens of thousands, his action would still fit the FBI's definition,

---

1. A first-century AD Romano-Jewish scholar, historian and hagiographer.
2. Georgios Patronos, *The History of Jesus (from the manger to the empty tomb)*, Athens: Domos Editions, 1991, p. 580ff.

according to which mass murder is the "killing of four or more persons during an event with no 'cooling-off period' between the murders". Consequently, Herod falls under this classification, as one of its grizzliest examples, as a children's mass murderer.

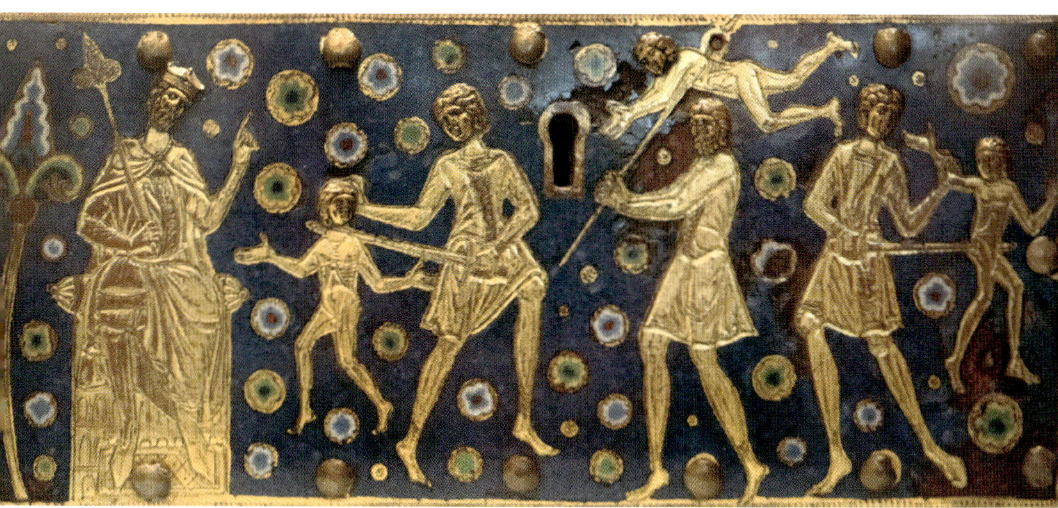

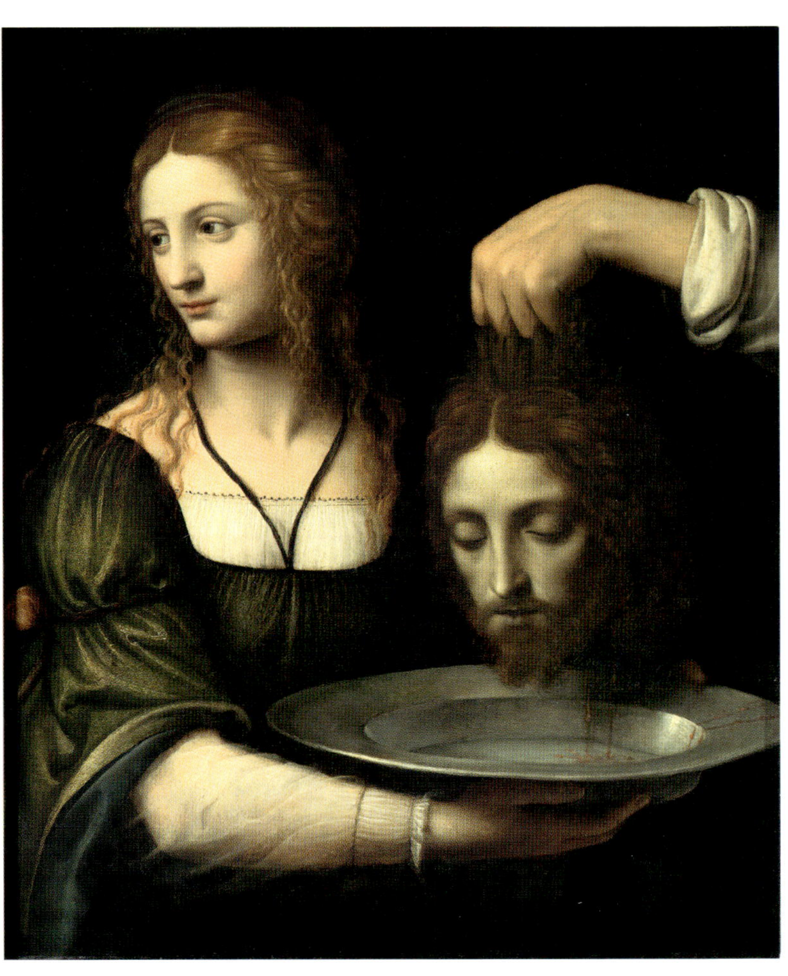

CHAPTER 6
THE UNWANTED REWARD

ABETTOR - FEMME FATALE

Bernardino Luini,
Salome with the Head of Saint John the Baptist,
date unknown, beginning 16th century
H: 62 cm; L: 55 cm

First Floor, Denon, Grand Gallery, Room 5

In some cases the person who physically murders another is not the only offender involved in the crime. The role of the "brain" and the "hand" in a murder can sometimes be distinguished. Thus enters the abettor, the person who commands, advises, instigates or encourages another person to commit a crime, sharing the criminal intent with which the crime was committed.[1]

Salome's biblical story[2] (like Judith's in the chapter entitled "The Seducer with the Sword") has been a source of inspiration for artists throughout the centuries. Yet, unlike Judith, Salome is not the heroic murderess. In John the Baptist's decapitation, Salome is considered the archetype of the Femme Fatale and an abettor par excellence. We will see, however, that the main culprit behind the saint's murder was another woman: Salome's mother.

John was the cousin of Christ. He had baptized Jesus in the River Jordan, thus his epithet "the Baptist". His sense of justice and outspoken nature landed him into trouble with Herod

1. *West's Encyclopedia of American Law*, 2nd edition, The Gale Group, Inc., 2008.

2. Her story is recounted in the Gospels of Matthew and Mark. Yet her name is not mentioned, she is simply referred as *Herodiade's daughter*.

Antipas. The latter was the tetrarch[1] of Galilee and Perea, where John would preach at the beginning of the 1st century AD. Herod Antipas was generally considered to be a fair ruler, but his personal life found its way into John's sermons, aimed against him. The reason? Having divorced his wife, Herod had married his brother's wife, Herodias.

John's preaching against the ruler could be summarized in one line *"It is not lawful for you to have your brother's wife"*. Despite Herod's warnings, John persisted in his judgment against him, resulting in his imprisonment. Yet, despite his wife Herodias' insistent demands, the tetrarch did not dare kill John, as he was beloved by the people of Galilee and he was actually speaking the truth.

In the meantime, Herodias looked for an opportunity to put an end to what she considered John's slanderous ranting. She was to find it during Herod's birthday celebration. Salome, Herodias' daughter from her first marriage, danced before him in such a sensual way, that the ruler promised her whatever she would ask of him as a reward. "I'd give you half my kingdom" he is said to have exclaimed in the heat and the drunkenness of the moment. The young Salome was blinded by the possibilities presented to her. She could ask for anything: money, jewels, palaces, power. Yet, when she consulted with her mother on the matter, Herodias demanded that she defend her honour: she was to ask for the saint's head!

Though Herod was distressed by Salome's demand, he was bound by his promise, made in public. There was no room to

1. The so-called Herodian Tetrarchy was formed after Herod the Great's death in 4 BC, dividing his kingdom between his sons as an inheritance. Herod Antipas was the ruler of Galilee and Perea until 34 AD.

back out. He kept his word, and the result is before us in this painting. A hand is coming out of the shadows, producing an even more sinister effect in the scene.[1] The executioner offers John the Baptist's freshly decapitated head to Salome on a silver platter. She will then present it to her mother, the real "brain" behind the deed.

We know she is rewarded for her sensuality, we know she is the archetype of the Femme Fatale, yet here she is presented in a modest dress. She poses no threat to the spectator.[2] In her indifference, Salome looks away, her face showing no sign of satisfaction or joy. She would have rather asked for another reward.

And yet this unwanted gift will burden her for the ages to come. Her mother's name will soon be forgotten. And in place of the true abettor behind John's murder, Salome will be forever referred to as such, considered in collective memory as the one with an innocent man's blood on her hands.

---

1. Théophile Gautier, *Guide de l'amateur au Musée du Louvre* (1867), Paris: Nabu Press, 2013.
2. F. A. Gruyer, *Voyage autour du Salon Carré au Musée du Louvre*, Paris, 1891.

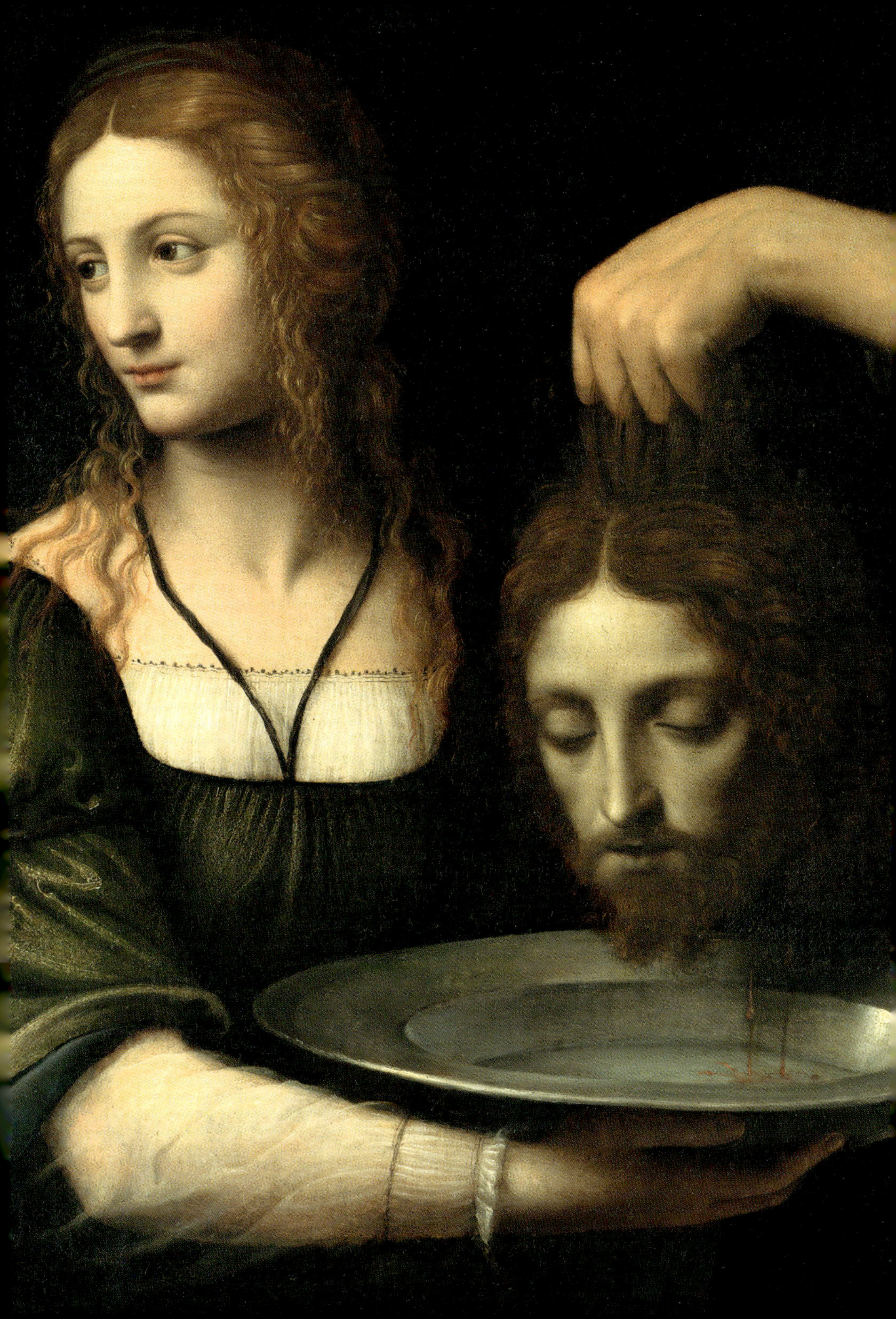

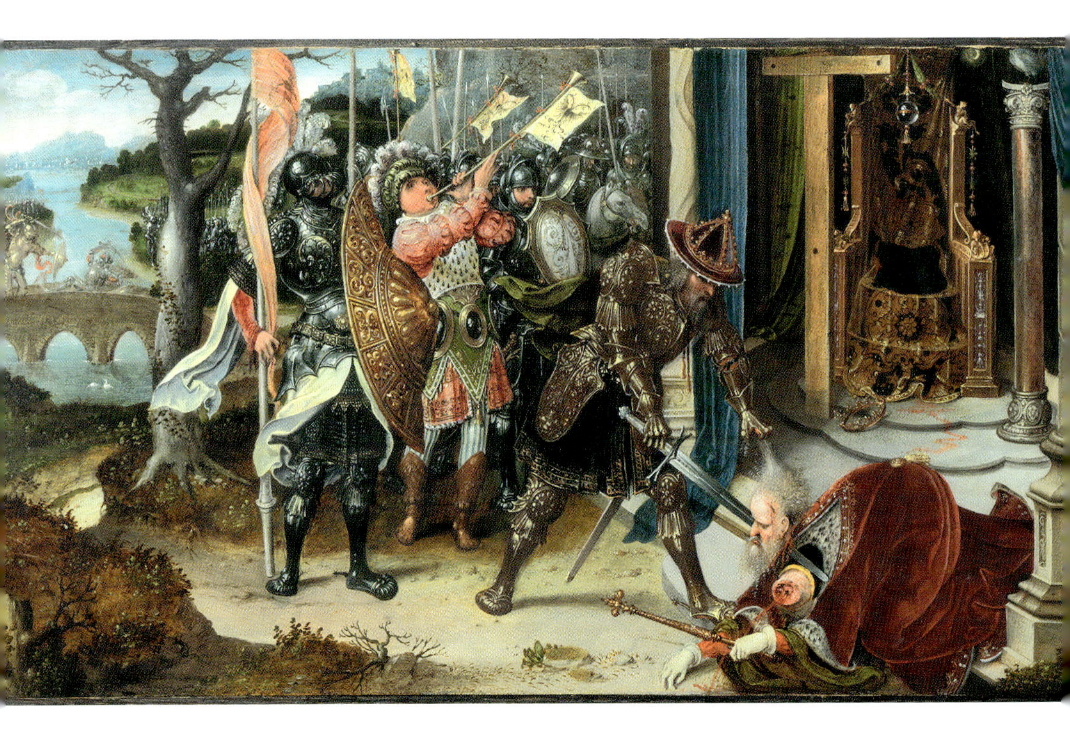

CHAPTER 7

IN THE NAME OF THE FATHER, THE SON, AND THE HOLY ROOSTER

BLASPHEMY · REGICIDE

Jan de Beer, *The Emperor Heraclius Decapitating Khosrow, King of the Persians*, about 1515–20
H: 24 cm; L: 42 cm

Second floor, Richelieu,
Netherlands, first half of the 16th century, Room 9

Byzantium is a civilization that, despite its almost thousand years of existence, is largely unfamiliar to Westerners. The Byzantine Empire was the extension of the Greek and Roman civilizations and at the same time a bearer of Christianity.[1] It was an artistic and philosophical lantern of light during Europe's Dark Ages. Protecting mainland Europe from Muslim attacks in the east, it provided Europe the space, time and seeds to prepare itself for the forthcoming Renaissance. Of course the passions and political intrigues that Byzantium is mainly known for, while only a small part of its history, are entirely true.

The triumphant sound of trumpets, bearing the yellow Byzantine flag with its black two-headed eagle, one facing west and the other east – fills our ears as we stand closer to this painting.

Who is this man in the exquisitely ornamented armour, holding the old Persian king's head in one hand and the de-capitating sword in the other? His name is Heraclius and he is the Emperor of Byzantium as well as its army's general. And getting there was no easy task.

The story goes as follows: In 602 AD, twenty-six years before the scene we are witnessing, a low-ranking army

1. Judith Herum, *Byzantium, The Surprising Life of a Medieval Empire*, Penguin Books Ltd, 2007.

officer named Phokas killed the reigning Byzantine Emperor Mauritius and took power. The new emperor was a cruel leader and soon earned the nicknames of Godless, Tyrant and Bloodthirsty. So when Heraclius, the son of the exarch[1] of Africa, conquered the Byzantine Empire's capital, Constantinople, and defeated Phokas in 610 AD, the people welcomed him as a liberator. Legend has it that when Heraclius was about to decapitate the former occupant of the throne, he asked him why he had reigned in such a cruel manner. Phokas replied with a cynical question: "Why, do you think you'll rule any better?"

When Heraclius took power the empire was crumbling. The army was broken up, the European provinces have been falling into the hands of Slavs, Avars and Lombards for years, and the eastern provinces were conquered from the Persians, one after the other. At their head was the Persian King Khosrow II. Earlier, in 590 AD, Khosrow, heir to his father's throne was overthrown by a coup and asked the Byzantine Emperor Mauritius for help. With the money and army provided by Mauritius, Khosrow succeeded in taking back the throne he was entitled to. From then on, the Persian king was Mauritius' friend and ally.

So when Mauritius was killed by Phokas in 602 AD, Khosrow found the pretext to attack the empire. Antioch and Damascus fell into Persian hands and thousands of Christians were slaughtered. When Jerusalem was also conquered, the True Cross, kept there since the time of Emperor Constantine, was taken to the Persian capital.

1. The ruler of a province in the Byzantine Empire.

In 618 AD, the Emperor Heraclius signed a humiliating treaty, with the Persian army just outside the walls of Constantinople. However, this treaty gave him the opportunity and the time to reorganize and reequip his army.

The painting illustrates the conclusion of Heraclius' campaign, which started in 622 AD, to re-conquer the provinces he had lost. In 628 AD, having crushed the Persian army at Nineveh, the old Assyrian capital, Heraclius apprehended Khosrow himself.

According to sources, the Persian king claimed to be God. In his palace he sat on a gilded throne, which was in constant 360-degree movement, mimicking the universe, ornamented with precious stones that represented stars and planets. Mocking the Christian doctrine of the Holy Trinity, he considered himself the Father. On his right, he placed the stolen True Cross, representing the Son. On his left perched a white rooster, representing the Holy Spirit, on a granite pillar. All this can be seen on the far right of the painting.[1]

Blasphemy, a capital offence at this time, would cost the Persian king his life. With Khosrow dead the eastern provinces returned to Byzantine rule, only to be captured by Muslims a few decades later. The True Cross was returned to Jerusalem.

As for the painting itself, it is not historically accurate, as Khosrow was overthrown and killed by his own son Kavadh II. Nevertheless, artists have the poetic license and liberty to deviate from the facts, edifying their representations of history, which is the case here.

As we walk away from the painting, the sound of trumpets subsides, but impressions of the spurting blood from

1. "*Héraclius décapitant Chosroes* de Jan de Beer", *Le tableau du mois*, no. 166.

Khosrow's neck will follow us, at least until the next blood-bath a few rooms away.

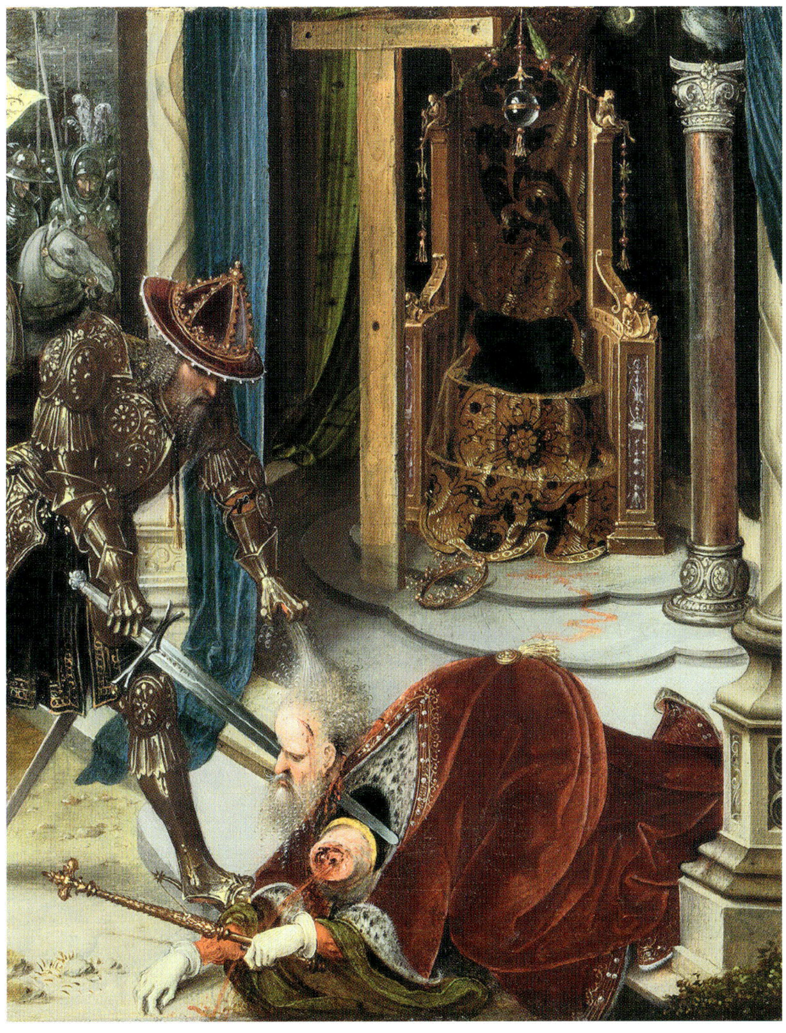

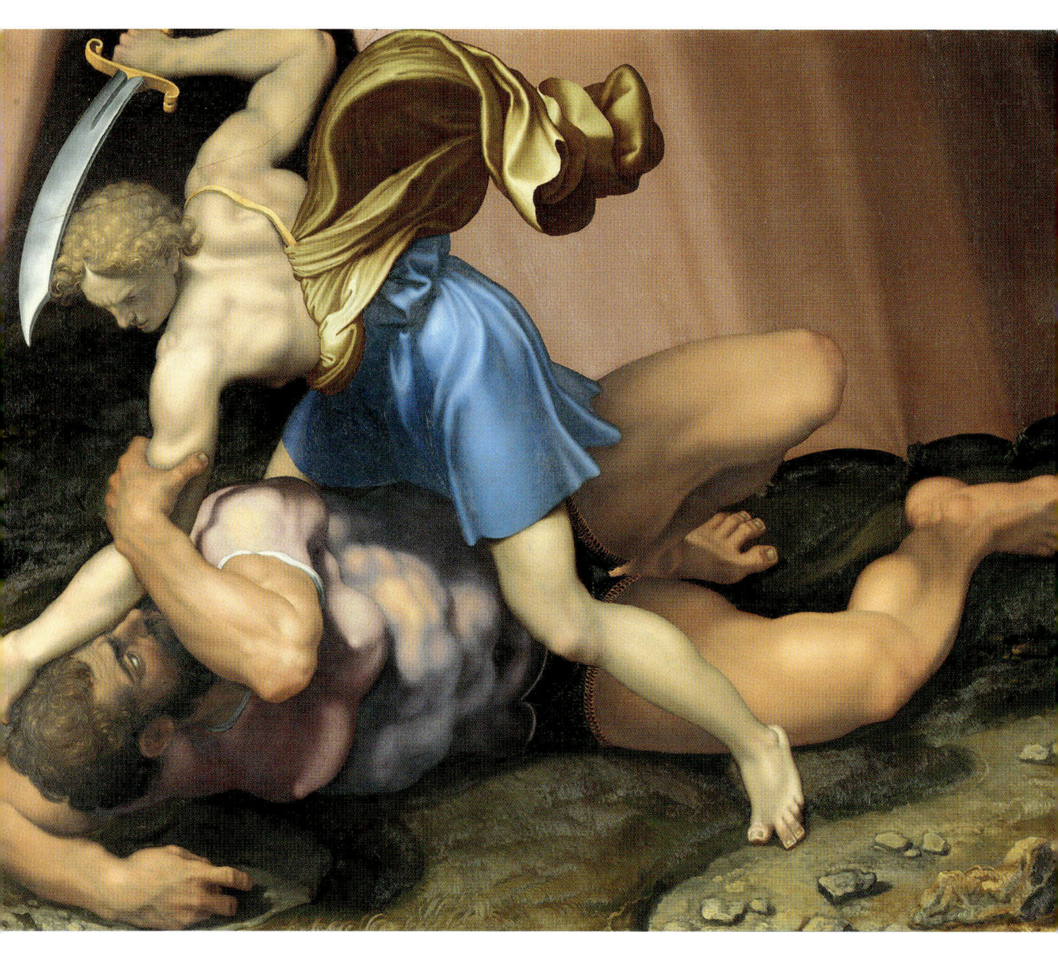

CHAPTER 8
ONE WAY OR ANOTHER

DUEL - SINGLE COMBAT

Daniele Ricciarelli, known as Daniele da Volterra,
David and Goliath, about 1550–55
Oil on slate, H: 133 cm; L: 172 cm
Recto and verso

First floor, Denon, Grand Gallery, Room 8

A duel is the formal battle to death that takes place at a prearranged time and place, between two persons, as a result of an earlier quarrel, in order to resolve a point of honour.[1] A single combat is the duel between two warriors in the context of a battle between two armies.[2] As we will see, a duel can be fought between people from different camps, but also between the notion of good and evil, between a teacher – representing the old – and his pupil – representing the new – even between two different art forms.

The work of art you're looking at here is unique within the museum. It is a "double-faced" painting, one that is painted on both sides of the slate, illustrating the same subject from a different angle. The work is by Danielle da Volterra, a close friend and disciple of Michelangelo. It depicts a famous scene from the Bible, the combat between David and Goliath that was to determine the outcome of the war between Israelites and Philistines. Yet the scene we witness is a result of poetic license and not described as such in the Bible. There was no physical battle between the two men in the Old Testament.

---

1. http://www.thefreedictionary.com/
2. Victor Morris Udwin, *Between Two Armies: The Place of the Duel in Epic Culture*, Brill, 1998.

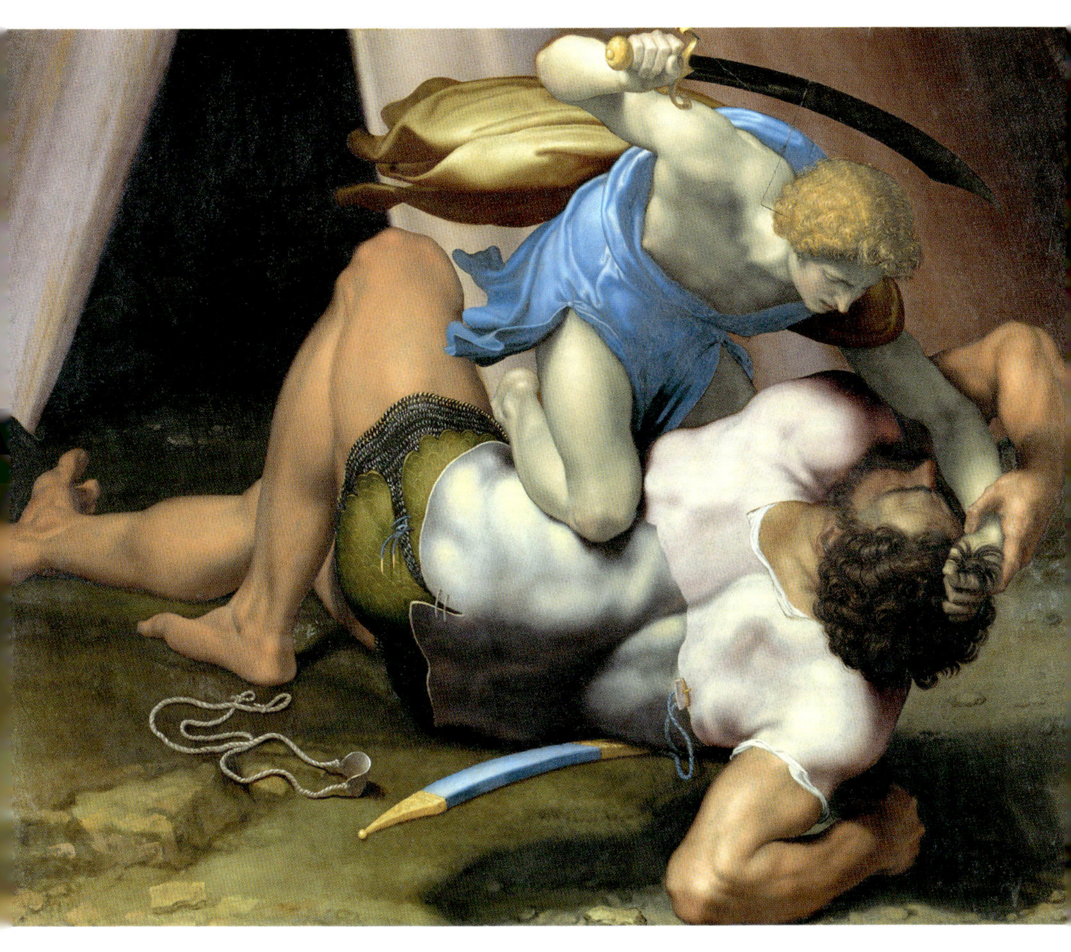

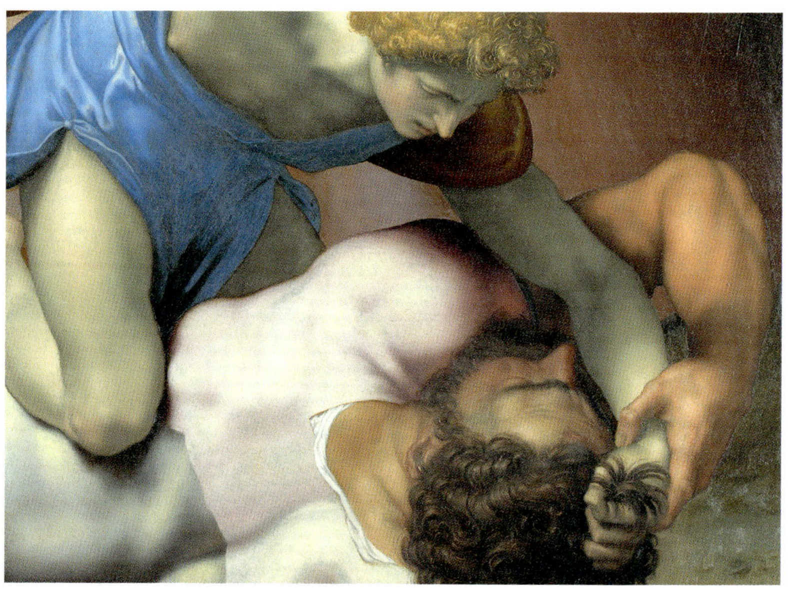

The backstory concerns two enemy camps in a face off. For forty days in a row, a nine-foot tall Philistine, Goliath, would appear in front of the Israelites and shout: "Choose a man and have him come down to me. If he is able to fight and kill me, we (the Philistines) will become your subjects; but if I overcome and kill him, you will become our subjects and serve us."[1]

No one was willing to face the giant Philistine, until a young shepherd named David appeared. His credentials were limited to killing lions and bears threatening his flock. And yet he stepped up to this lofty challenge, he fought and, using his sling, struck the Philistine on the forehead with a stone. We

1. 1 Samuel 1, the Old Testament.

can see his weapon in the painting (*Side B*). The giant has fallen to the ground. David goes on to decapitate Goliath with his own sword and the Israelites win the war.

On *Side A* we see the small David on top of the Philistine. His angry look is aimed at his enemy, who lies defeated. His sword's tip is directed at the giant's head. Yet Goliath's posture seems calm. Too calm. The giant could have easily tossed aside David. However, even though his left hand grasps his enemy, his right hand lies limp and motionless on the ground.

The passivity of the Philistine becomes clearer on *Side B* of the painting. At first glance, we seem to find the exact same moment but from a different angle. We can see the murder weapon, the sling laying next to the fallen giant's body. But take a closer look: it's not just the same scene from another point of view. There is a small, yet distinctive time lapse between the two sides.[1]

We see the that the duelling protagonists' heads are closer together. The sword's position is changed and David's grasp on Goliath's hair is tighter. In addition, Goliath's hand on David has shifted to his wrist, and seems looser. The giant's legs also seem more relaxed, his muscles show no tension. The battle is about to end and David's expression is no longer angry, while the Philistine looks ready to surrender to his fate.

The duel between them, represents more than the battle between the Israelites and the Philistines, between "good" and "evil". It serves as an instrument in another form of duel, one between two art forms.

---

1. Vincent Delieuvin, "Daniele de Volterra, Les deux faces d'un chef-d'œuvre," *Grande Galerie*, no. 17, Sept.-Oct.-Nov. 2011.

During the Renaissance, a theoretical conflict for superiority raged between proponents of painting and sculpture. Michelangelo, Da Volterra's master, claimed the only way to resolve this question, known as the "paragon polemic"[1] was for the same artist, an expert in both art forms, to represent the same subject in both painting and sculpture. Too old to do the work himself, Michelangelo appointed his loyal pupil Da Volterra to undertake this challenge. The work before us with its two sides and detailed body postures is the painting "duelist". It's opponent, a clay sculpture, was unfortunately lost. As a result we shall never know the resolution to this artistic duel.[2]

If we dig a little deeper, another duel is revealed, a more personal one. It is a conflict between the new and the old. Da Volterra was one of Michelangelo's closest disciples and the master's influence on Da Volterra's work is significant. This along with Michelangelo's alleged homosexuality[3] and the attraction a "protégé" pupil may feel for his teacher, can lead us to see the painting from a completely different point of view.

We notice a complicity between the two characters. Goliath's surrendered pose and the expression on David's face, at the moment before killing him, seem sexually charged. Their two faces come closer as if about to kiss. The sword case under Goliath's body can be seen as an erection. David represents the student, in a love-hate relationship with his master, the artistic giant, the great talent. He is attached to

1. Daniel Soulié, *Louvre secret et insolite*, Paris: Parigramme Editions, 2011.

2. Vincent Delieuvin, "Quand la peinture s'attaque à la sculpture. Le combat de David et Goliath par Daniele de Volterra", *Grande Galerie*, no. 3, March-April-May 2008, no. 3.

3. Sigmund Freud, Correspondence (1935), in Kevin Lewes, *The psychoanalytic theory of male homosexuality*, New York: Simon and Schuster, 1988.

him, attracted by his work and personality, yet he needs to "kill" him in order to acquire his own existence, his own personal glory. David represents the new, Goliath stands for the old, the master whose influence Da Volterra needs to be freed from. A talent who needs to conquer another – superior – talent.

Unlike the outcome of the duel between David and Goliath the conflict between the two art forms is still unresolved. In the battle between the master and the pupil, it was Michelangelo who was the victor. Yet this work underscores the pupil's virtuosity, though under the constant shadow of his master.

The "Battle between David and Goliath", was offered to Louis XIV in 1715, as a diplomatic gift; it was presented to the king as a painting by Michelangelo.[1]

1. Correspondence of the Directors of the Académie de France in Rome with the Surintendants des Bâtiments, Anatole de Montaignon and Jules Guiffrey, Paris, 1893.

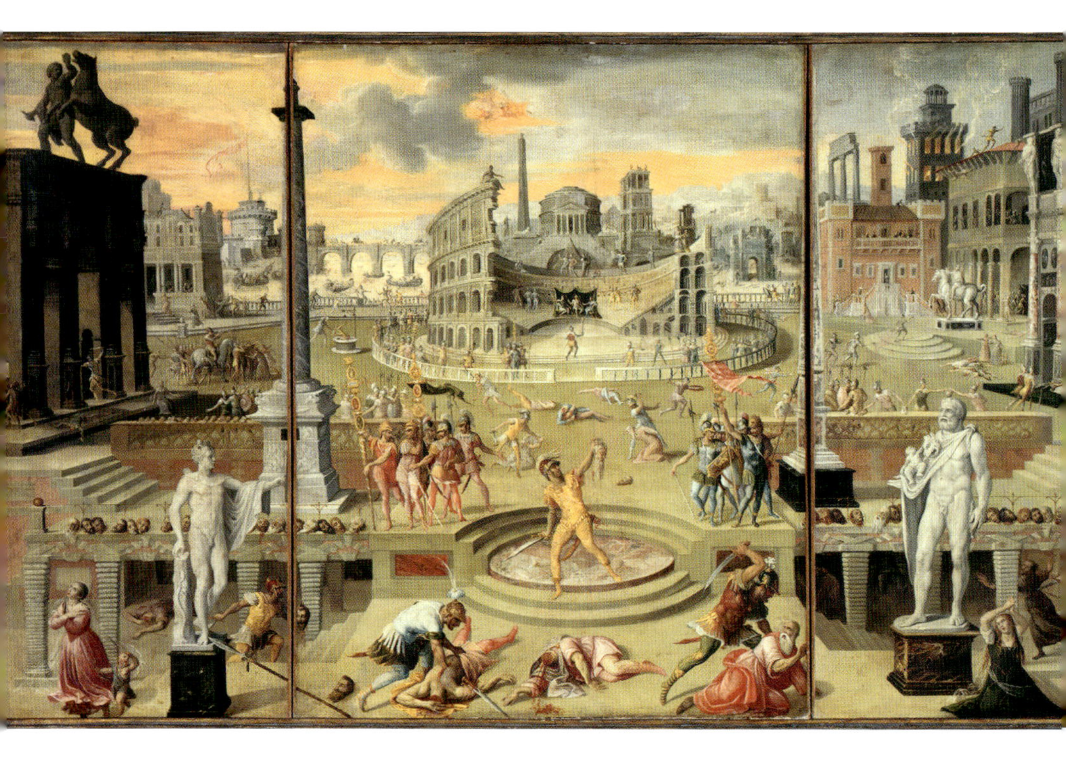

CHAPTER 9
A RECURRING NIGHTMARE

POLITICAL MASSACRE - PROSCRIPTIONS

Antoine Caron, *Massacre of the Triumvirate*, 1566
H: 116 cm; L: 195 cm

Second floor, Richelieu, Cousin and Caron, Room 9

Artists often hide truths between images and symbols. So when we are able to read between the lines and go beyond the obvious, we can decode their intended meaning. This principle is applied to the painting we have before us. The ancient Roman political massacre from the 1st century BC that we see here, is a masked reference to contemporary events during the time of the French painter, in the 16th century.

At first glance, this painting, with its warm colours and idyllic light resembles what could have been a postcard from ancient Rome. Every cliché of the Eternal City is featured on the triptych.[1] We see the Coliseum in the centre with the Pantheon behind it, the Arc of Titus and Hadrian's Mausoleum on the left, all encircled by the Tiber River in the background.

Yet, a closer look reveals something less idyllic. Between the magnificent buildings and the pink and yellow colours of the sunset, frenzy prevails.[2] Before our eyes, a massacre is being committed: several defenceless people are killed simultaneously, indiscriminately and cruelly. Its motives here are political and its actors are three rulers, fitting into the definition of political massacre.[3]

---

1. *Bulletin de la société de l'histoire de l'art français*, 1940, Librairie Colin, 1941. p.18.
2. "La Renaissance", *Peinture Française I*, Librairie Larousse, 1942, pp.49–51.
3. Melson, Robert, "Theoretical Inquiry into the Armenian Massacres of 1894–1896" (July 1982). *Comparative Studies in Society and History* 24 (3) pp.482–83.

In the centre of the middle panel a man dressed in a yellow uniform, taller than every other figure in this painting, holds a head as a trophy. He defines what the painting is all about. The victim's freshly decapitated body is lying before him. But he's not the only one. On each side, on top of a wall sit dozens of heads, while other victims are about to be decapitated. No one is safe. No man, no woman, not even children.

On the lower part of the central panel, a soldier on our left has dipped his hand into a headless corpse's chest, looking for his heart. On our right, another soldier is about to strike an old man. On each extremity of the triptych, a woman is praying for her life. The woman on our left, under the statue of Apollo of Belvedere, is begging for her child's life to be spared.

Death is omnipresent in every corner of this tableau. A man is thrown into a well in the background. Just to the right of the Coliseum, heads are being passed from one soldier to another. In the middle of the right panel, a fire rages and men attempt to flee via the rooftops, or (further back in the left panel) by boat on the Tiber River.

The title tells us that we are witnessing the Massacre of the Triumvirate.[1] But who are the three men forming the group responsible for this bloodbath? Who are the leaders behind this mass killing? Judging from the background, the splendour or ancient Rome, we could imagine Marc Anthony, Marcus Lepidus and Octavian were involved.

After Julius Caesar's murder by Brutus, the three formed a coalition and fought against his assassins. The final battle took

1. A coalition of three magistrates or rulers for joint administration.

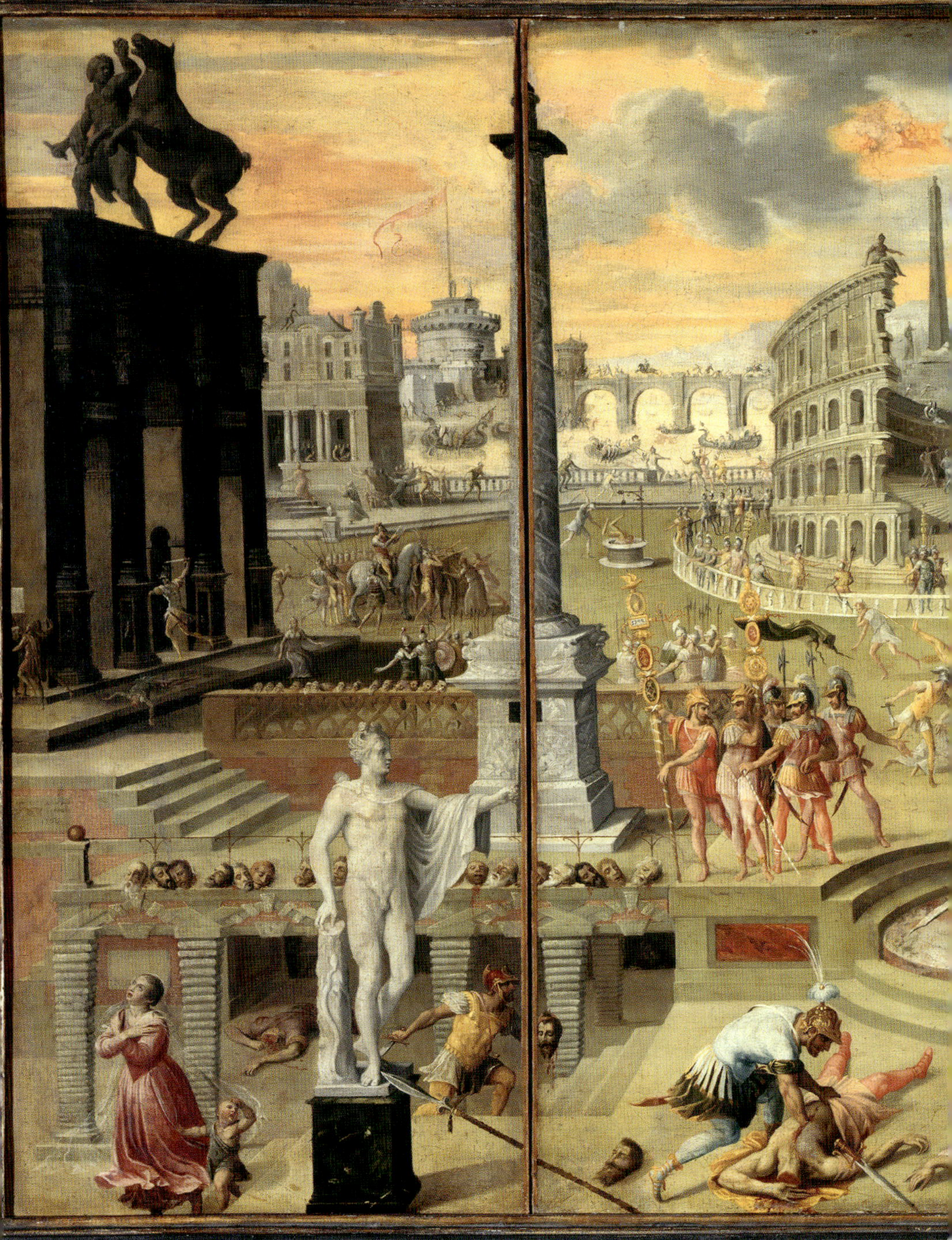

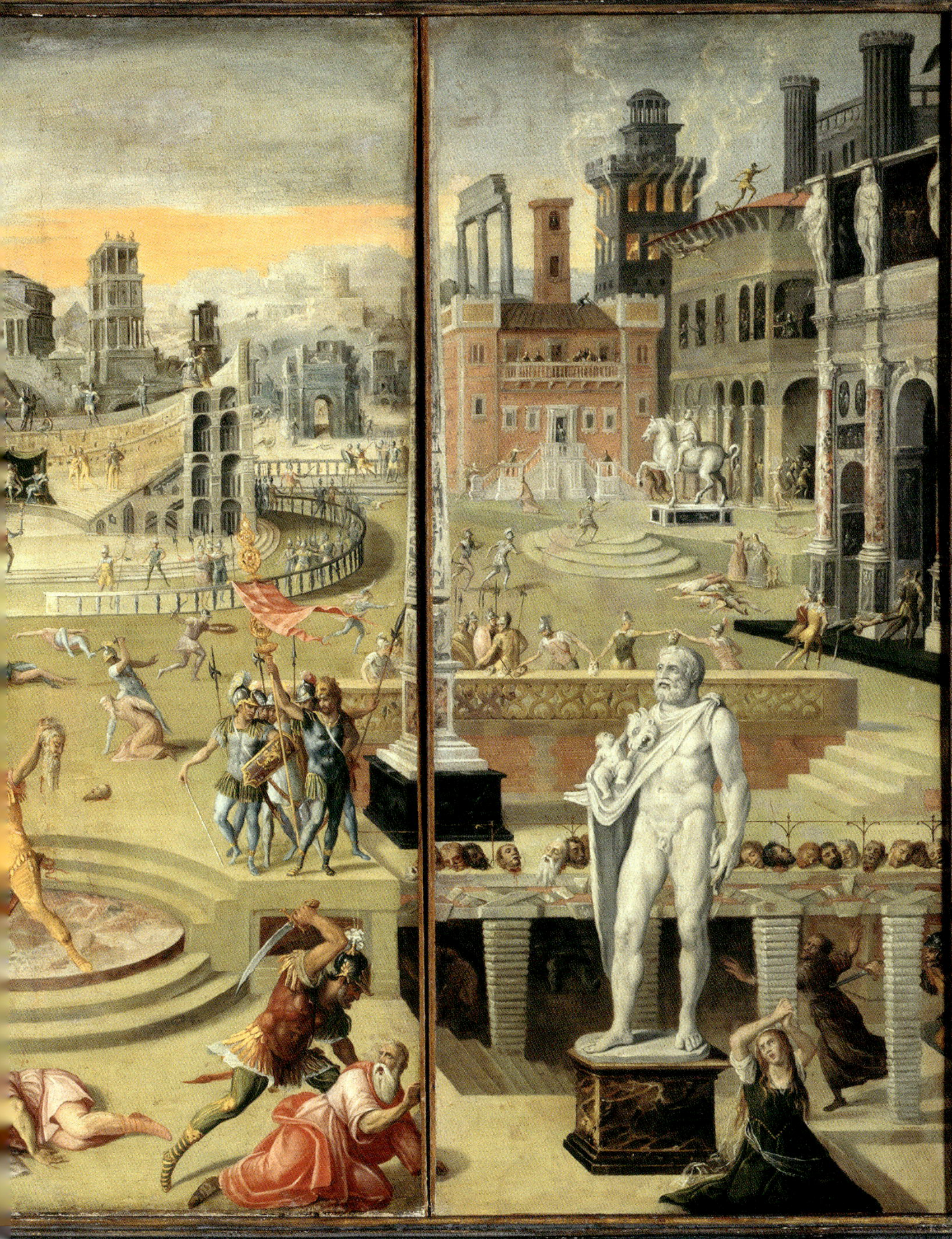

place in Greece, in Philippi, where the three men's forces won.[1] When they returned victorious to Rome, they killed whoever had supported the traitors. The mass political killings we witness took place in 42 BC. They are the outcome of the so-called Proscriptions, a decree condemning to death without a trial, all the enemies of the state.

Within the Coliseum, under a tent we see the three rulers, gazing upon the outcome of their orders. Meanwhile a soldier offers them a head and a pair of hands on his sword.

Yet, behind this ancient Roman scene, behind the obvious horror, an equally terrible scene plays out. A truth is concealed by the artist, which is about the time in which he lived. The theme is not about the Triumvirate consisting of the Roman Generals and their proscriptions. Or not *just* about this.[2]

Rather it concerns another group of three men, who formed a Catholic Triumvirate in France in 1561. They were Francois de Guise, Anne de Montmorency and Jacques d'Albon de St. Andre, the kingdom's most powerful men. Their motives were religious, with the French Protestants, the so-called Huguenots as victims. Between two and four million Protestants are believed to have lost their lives during the massacres of the Wars of Religion in France, from 1562 to 1598. This painting, created in 1566 may allude to the then recent massacre of Vassy, which took place on the 1 March 1562, when close to one hundred Huguenots were killed by De Guise.

---

1. Appian, *Roman History. The Civil Wars*, Book IV.
2. Exh. cat., *L'École de Fontainebleau*, Paris: Grand Palais, 1972, p.31.

It might also indicate a premonition of a future massacre[1] of a much bigger scale. On 24 August 1572, six years after this painting was completed, the Massacre of the Night of Saint Bartholomew began inside the Louvre Palace. It spread across Paris and then the whole of France (see chapter "Sacred Night, Bloody Night"). The scene before us resembles what one would have witnessed on that night, when more than three thousand people were killed in Paris.

This *mise en scene* serves as a metaphor of every massacre, regardless of motives, be they political, religious or other and regardless of the time, be it ancient or in the 21st century.

1. Michel Leiris, "Une peinture d'Antoine Caron", *Documents*, 1929.

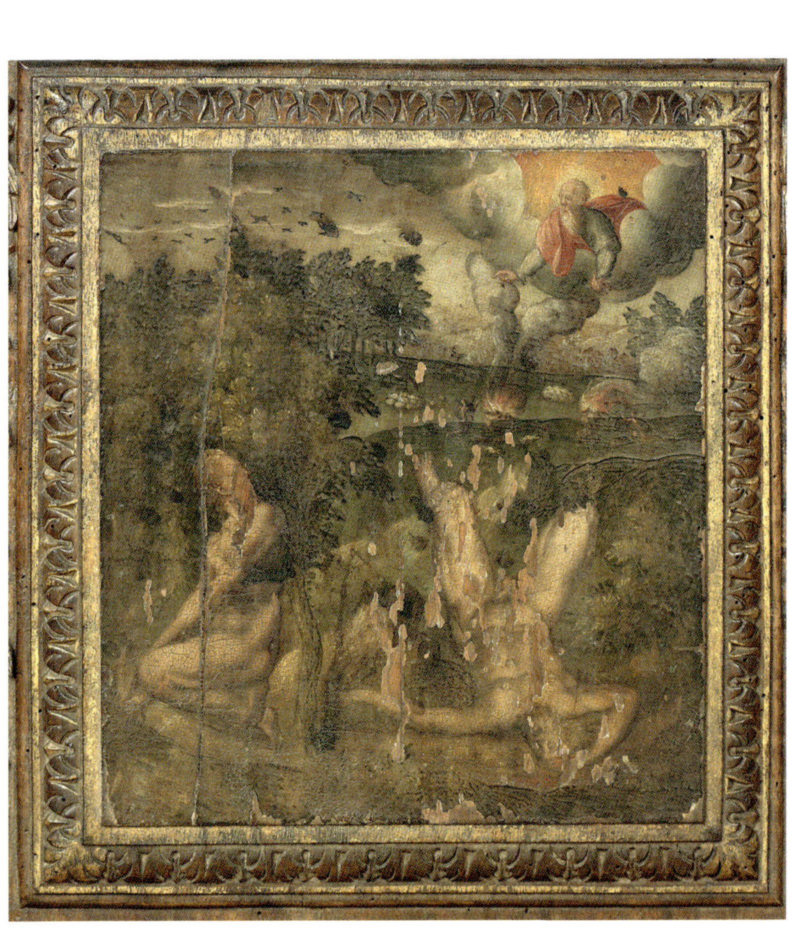

CHAPTER 10
OUR ANCESTOR, THE FIRST MURDERER

FRATRICIDE - PHYSIOGNOMIC THEORIES

Cain and Abel, France, about 1580
Lower part of a cabinet
Walnut, partially gilded and painted oak,
H: 206 cm; L: 150 cm; D: 60 cm

First Floor, Richelieu, François Ier, Room 16

This 16th-century armoire, delicately decorated – as if embroidered – with carved flowers and figures has a painted panel on each of its sections. It is a utilitarian object for everyday use and also a work of art.

To appreciate its two painted panels, sit on the floor and bring your eyes to the level of its lower half. Despite its cracks, scratches and faded colours, on the right panel we can still see the representation of humanity's first murder. And it is not just a man killing another man. What we see before us is the first fratricide, brother killing brother. Cain, the first-born son of Adam and Eve, is the murderer of their second-born, Abel.

All the elements of the Old Testament story are here, on a tiny picture of about 20 x 20 cm: In the background we see two fires serving as the brothers' offerings to God. Cain, working the soil, offered fruit and Abel who was a shepherd (we can distinguish sheep in the background, next to his fire), offered a generous portion of his flock. We can see the smoke from Abel's offering rising towards the sky, having been accepted by God. The smoke from Cain's offering, having been judged insufficient, is dispersed with the wind.

Cain became angry by God's rejection. After all he was the first-born and *he* should be God's blessed one. Come to think of it, why make offerings to a God that had thrown them out of Paradise for the Original Sin his parents, and not he, had committed.

In his fury, Cain took his brother out to the field and killed him with a stone. We see Abel's body lying lifeless, his hand still on his head where the stone had struck him. The look of shock and pain is frozen on his face.

Cain has his back to his victim, when God appears within the clouds. The murderer's hands are hidden between his knees, as if denying his actions.

"Where is your brother, Abel?" the Lord asks. Cain turns his face towards his maker and replies, "I don't know. Am I my brother's keeper?"[1] This is the scene we are witnessing.

But God knows what has happened. "Listen! Your brother's blood cries out to me from the ground". And with that God exiled Cain from His lands. In response, Cain lamented "My punishment is more that I can bear [...] I will be a restless wanderer on the Earth and whoever finds me will kill me".

Then "God put a mark on Cain, so that no one who found him would kill him".

Cain was humanity's first murderer. And Cain's "mark of a murderer" was said to have been passed on to his children, who also inherited their father's killer instincts. This has been the basis, or the pretext of many physiognomic theories (more or less pseudoscientific) claiming that we are able to identify potential killers by their physical characteristics.

1. Genesis 4:9, the Old Testament.

As you leave this macabre scene to continue your tour in the museum, stop and think: if Cain was the first human to father children after Adam, aren't we all related to him? Aren't we all Cain's children? Aren't we all, therefore, potential murderers?

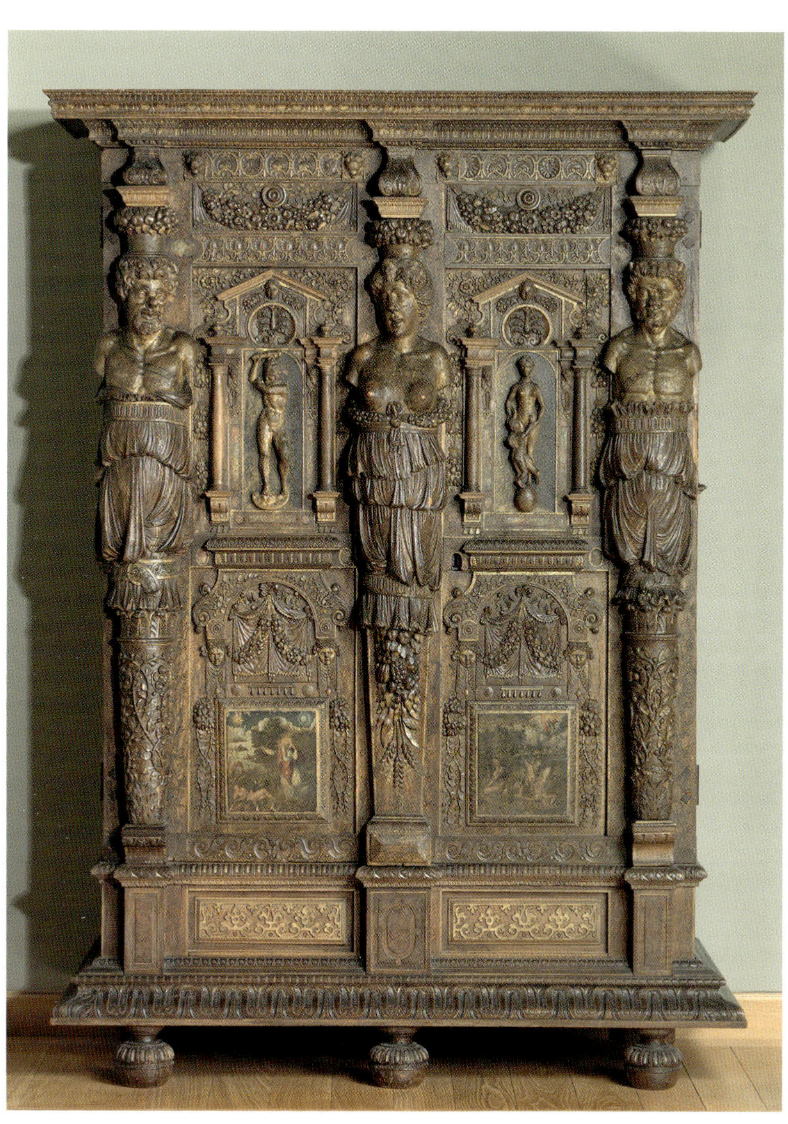

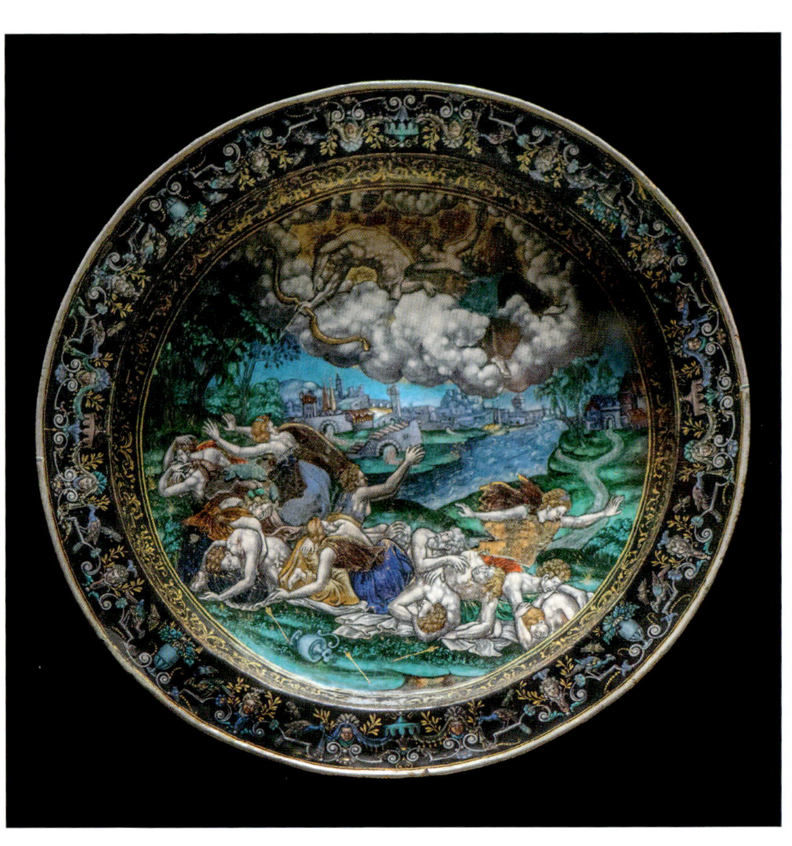

CHAPTER 11
A FAMILY VENDETTA

VENDETTA - MASSACRE

Martial Courteys, *The Massacre of the Niobids*,
Limoges, late 16th century
Platter, painted enamel on copper,
D: 46.5 cm; H: 5.4 cm

First Floor, Richelieu, Gallery of the Hunts of Maximilian, Room 19

The word vendetta derives from the Latin word *vindicta,* meaning vengeance. Vendettas are blood feuds, between social groups or families, usually based on resentment, when one of the parties involved feels (justifiably or not) that their honour, status or life has been threatened or attacked by the other.

In Greek mythology, the "twin gods" Apollo and his sister Artemis loved and protected their mother, Leto. Their sensibility is justified, considering what she had endured in order to give birth to them (see chapter "Mommy Dearest"). So when her honour was at stake, they would go to extremes in order to protect it.

Additionally when the ancient Greek notion of hubris[1] is applied to the equation, things can only get worse.

Before us is the frantic scene of a massacre in progress, the brutal slaughter of many people, as the result of a vendetta, based on family honour. On the lower half of this plate, we see a group of victims. Some are lying on the ground, others are running in an attempt to escape or protect their siblings from an attack that comes from above. These fourteen figures, dead

1. Extreme pride or self confidence, defying moral and divine rules.

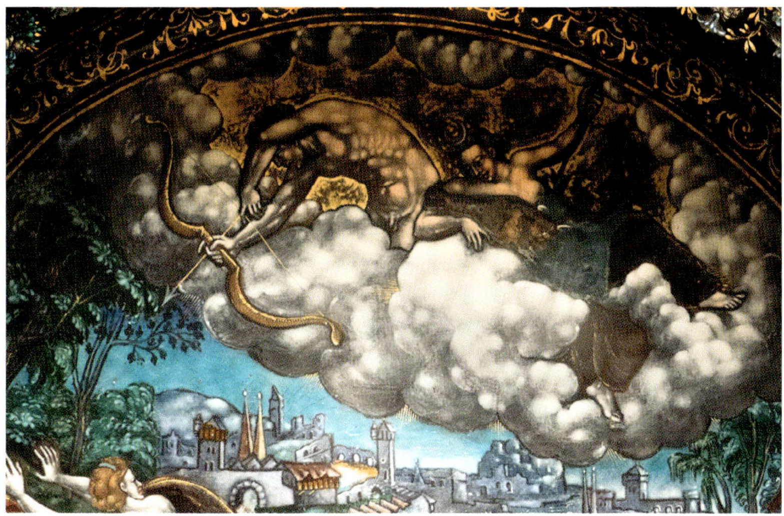

or about to die, are the Niobids – the seven sons and seven daughters of Niobe, wife of the King of Thebes.[1]

On the upper part of the scene, within a cloud, we see those responsible for this mass killing: Apollo, with his bow and arrows, slaying the male children and Artemis[2] with her spear, about to finish off the girls of this unfortunate family.[3]

It was Niobe's hubristic boastings about her offspring that caused their demise. Having come from Phrygia[4] to Thebes, she was not accustomed to the city's religious conventions. So when the annual celebration in Leto's honour was being held, she addressed the crowd and, with an air of arrogance, she

1. Thebes was the largest city of the ancient region of Boeotia in Central Greece.

2. Diana in Roman mythology.

3. Sophie Baratte, *Les Émaux peints de Limoges*, Réunion des Musées Nationaux, 2000, p. 364.

4. An ancient kingdom in the west central part of Anatolia, in what is now Turkey.

criticized them: "What a foolishness this is: to worship beings you have never seen, instead of those who stand before your eyes. I am the daughter and the wife of kings, but most of all I am seven times more fertile than Leto with only two children. I have fourteen! So, worship me, as fortunate I am and fortunate I shall remain!"

Hubris in ancient Greece was always followed by Nemesis, in other words divine punishment. So insulting the twin gods' mother was ill advised. The moment her cocky speech was over, clouds gathered over Thebes and a rain of arrows and spears fell upon her children standing by her. No one would survive.

Niobe's husband having witnessed his fourteen children being killed and knowing he could not carry out a vendetta against the gods, committed suicide. Niobe returned to Phrygia and, due to her profound grief, turned into stone.

If you visit Mount Sipylus in modern-day Turkey, locals will tell you about the Weeping Rock. Rainwater seeps through the porous limestone of this natural rock formation – which resembles a woman's face. It is said to be Niobe, eternally shedding her tears for her massacred children.

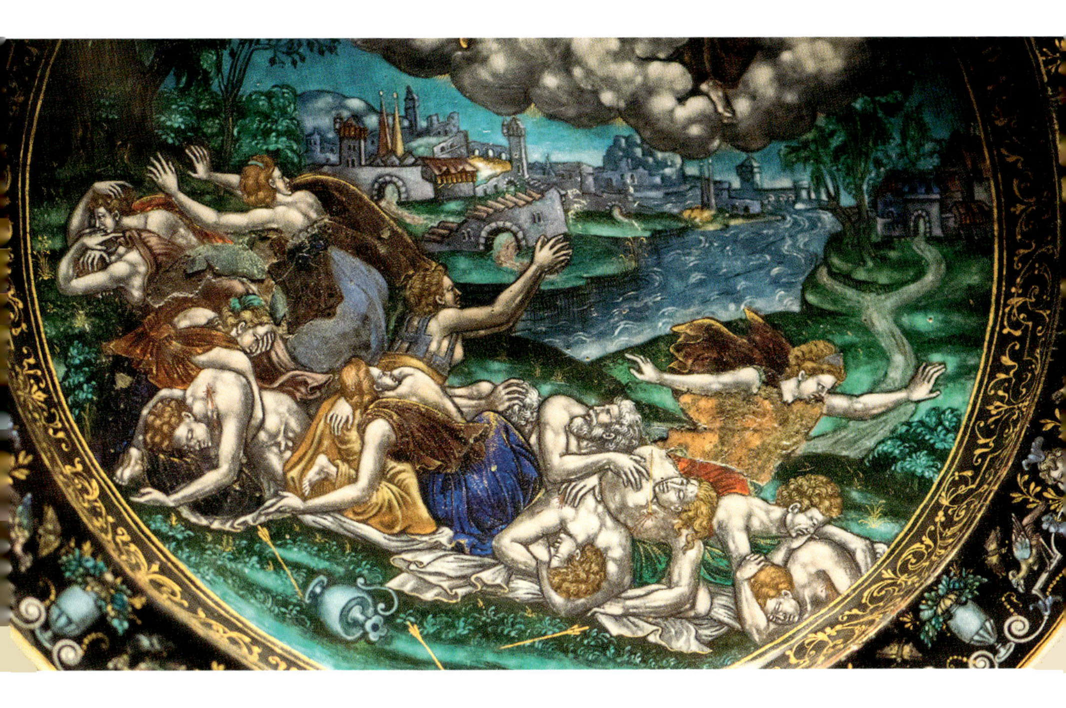

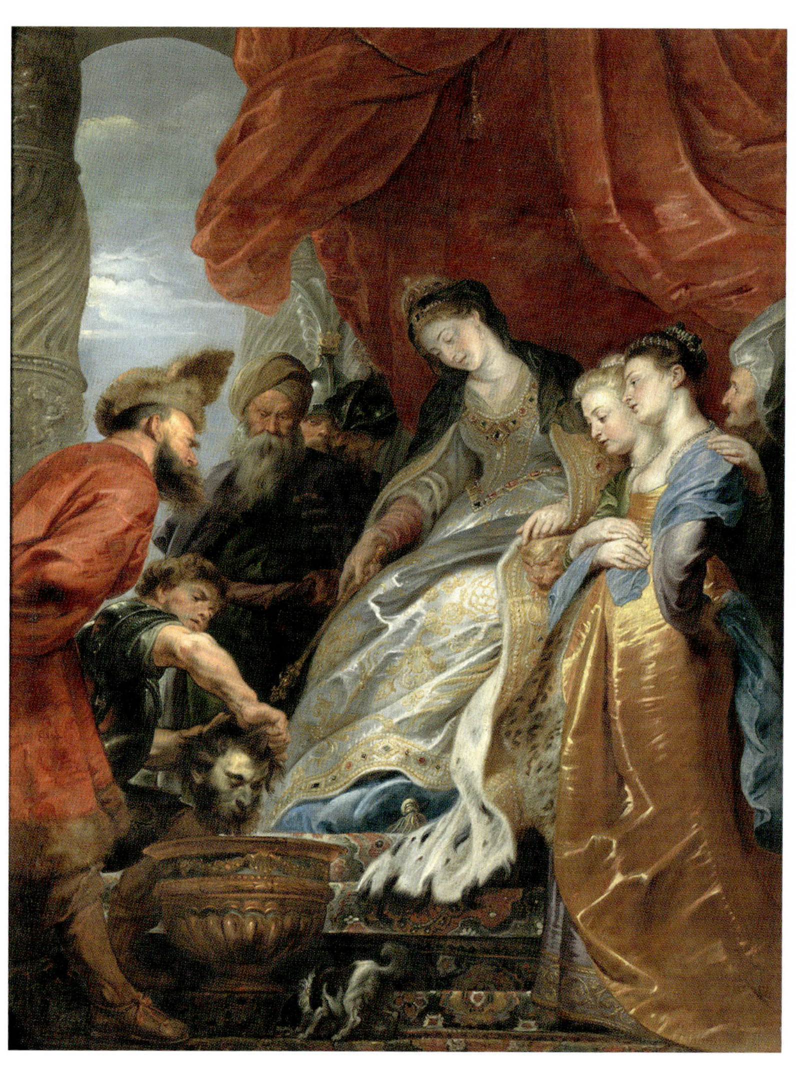

CHAPTER 12
A MOTHER'S REVENGE

WOMEN WHO KILL - REVENGE KILLING

Petrus Paulus Rubens,
Thomyris Having the Head of Cyrus the Great Plunged into a Vessel Full of Blood, to Avenge her Son's Death, about 1620–25
H: 263 cm; L: 199 cm

Second floor, Richelieu,
Rubens and 17th-century Flemish painting, Room 17

Standing before this painting, we can almost hear the blood drops making a hollow noise as they escape the vessel and touch the carpeted floor. This is the only sound in the scene, as the crowd surrounding their queen waits in silence for the head of Cyrus to be plunged into the vase. The metallic smell of blood fills their nostrils.

The Persian king's name is known in history. Yet, not many know of the woman who is presented here by Rubens in an ensemble that resembles a Renaissance royal court rather than an ancient kingdom.

It is Herodotus, the ancient Greek historian that tells us her story.[1] And as with the ancient Greek worldview, the tale is not just about recounting facts. There's always a moral in the story and a higher truth to be learned.

Cyrus the leader of the greatest empire known up to the 6th century BC, was renowned as the Superman, the King of the World, the son of Luck and the brother of Victory. Most of all he was known to be invincible. All his lofty titles however did not help him when he decided to conquer the land of the Massagetae, a Scythian tribe situated north-east of the

1. Herodotus, *Histories,* 1.204.1 -1.2014.5.

Caspian Sea in central Asia, and ruled by a woman named Thomyris.

Cyrus had demanded her hand in marriage, and her land as dowry. Thomyris reading between the lines, understood that he was only interested in taking her fertile land, and refused. So, according to Herodotus, Cyrus camped on the other side of the Araxes River and started building a wooden bridge for his army to cross into the Massagetae land. The queen warned him to stop. His imminent attack was unfair and unjust, and whoever went against moral justice would meet with a bad ending. Her warnings were dismissed as a sign of a woman's weak nature.

Consequently, Thomyris invited Cyrus to choose where the battle would take place. As he could not allow an enemy – much less a female one – to step foot on his lands, he chose that the war would be fought in hers. Furthermore, Cyrus chose not to fight as fair-play demands. Justice is applied even in war, a fact the Persian king ignored, using tactics that were unworthy to a king, a man, a warrior.

When he reached Thomyris' land he set a trap. Banquets of food and wine were prepared and he instructed his army to temporarily retreat. The Massagetae, unaccustomed to wine, became drunk and soon lay unconscious on the ground. It was then child's play for Cyrus to attack and kill or capture more than half of Thomyris' army. Amongst the captured was General Spargapises, the queen's son.

When Thomyris learned what had happened, she demanded that Cyrus withdraw, as he was already victorious over half of her army, and release her son. After all Spargapises was not a true war prisoner but a victim of Cyrus' underhanded tricks.

If he did not agree to her terms, Thomyris swore on the Sun (the Massagetae's main deity) that she would literally quench his thirst for blood. Despite her threat, Cyrus did not relent. Furthermore, he helped Spargapises, embarrassed by his capture, to commit suicide.

This was the catalyst for Thomyris and the rest of her army to go into a frenzied battle against the Persian army. As history has its own moral code, Cyrus the invincible was defeated, killed and decapitated by the queen herself. He was the prey of a revenge killing, exacting punishment for a wrong, in a resentful or vindictive spirit.[1]

In the scene before us, Thomyris is about to fulfil her promise. She is seconds away from having her enemy's head plunged into a vessel full of blood, quenching his thirst. His head is beneath her feet. Her position is higher not only literally, but also metaphorically in the moral scale. She is the one who has "Right" on her side.

The blood that will soon spill over the vase will become one with the scarlet fabric extending from the curtain to the servant's attire and to the queen's red sleeve.

All eyes are fixed on the head about to be dipped in the vase. Cyrus' lips come together, as if about to drink from the vessel. The only one not looking at the vase is the old maid on the far right of the painting. Her eyes are fixed on her queen's face. Perhaps she was the one that raised her, or her dead son. She could be the mother of a man who died in battle, so she might be the only one who understands what's going on in Thomyris' mind right now: the feeling that revenge, no matter

1. dictionary.reference.com/browse/revenge

how justified, cannot bring back her dead son. She may even be the only witness to Thomyris' words, whispered as the head disappears within the scarlet pond "I might have killed you, but you have destroyed me".

This painting was part of Louis XIV's private collection. It was hung in the Throne Room to the left of the throne,[1] opposite the Sun King's famous portrait by Hyacinthe Rigaud. It served as an everyday reminder that the thirst to conquer has a limit. And this limit is not imposed by weapons, armies or human laws. This limit is of divine origin, dictated by Justice and Moral Law.

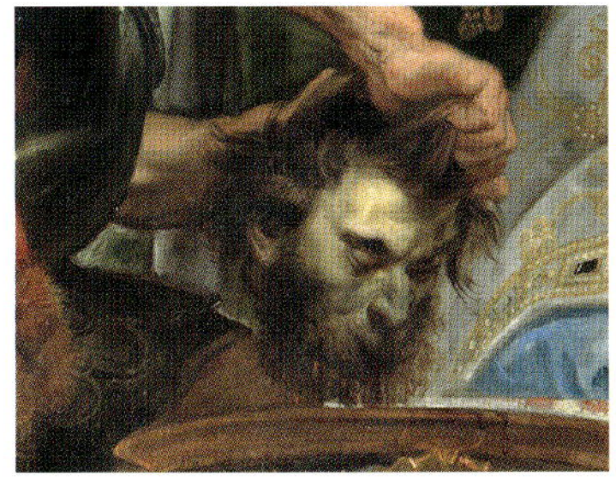

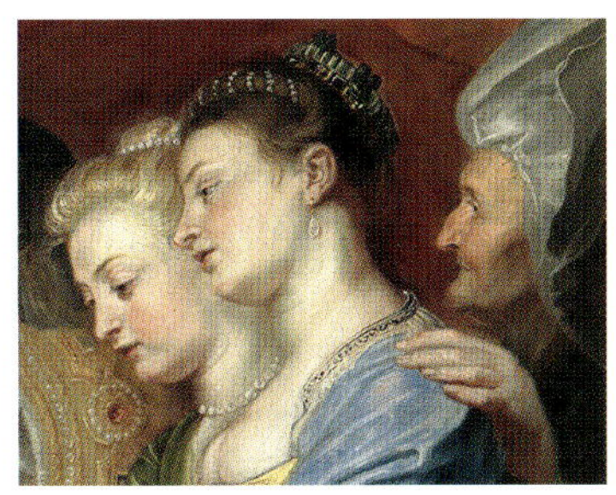

1. Robert W. Berger, "Queen Thomyris with the Head of Cyrus", Bulletin of the Museum of Fine Arts Boston, vol. 77, 1979, pp. 20–21.

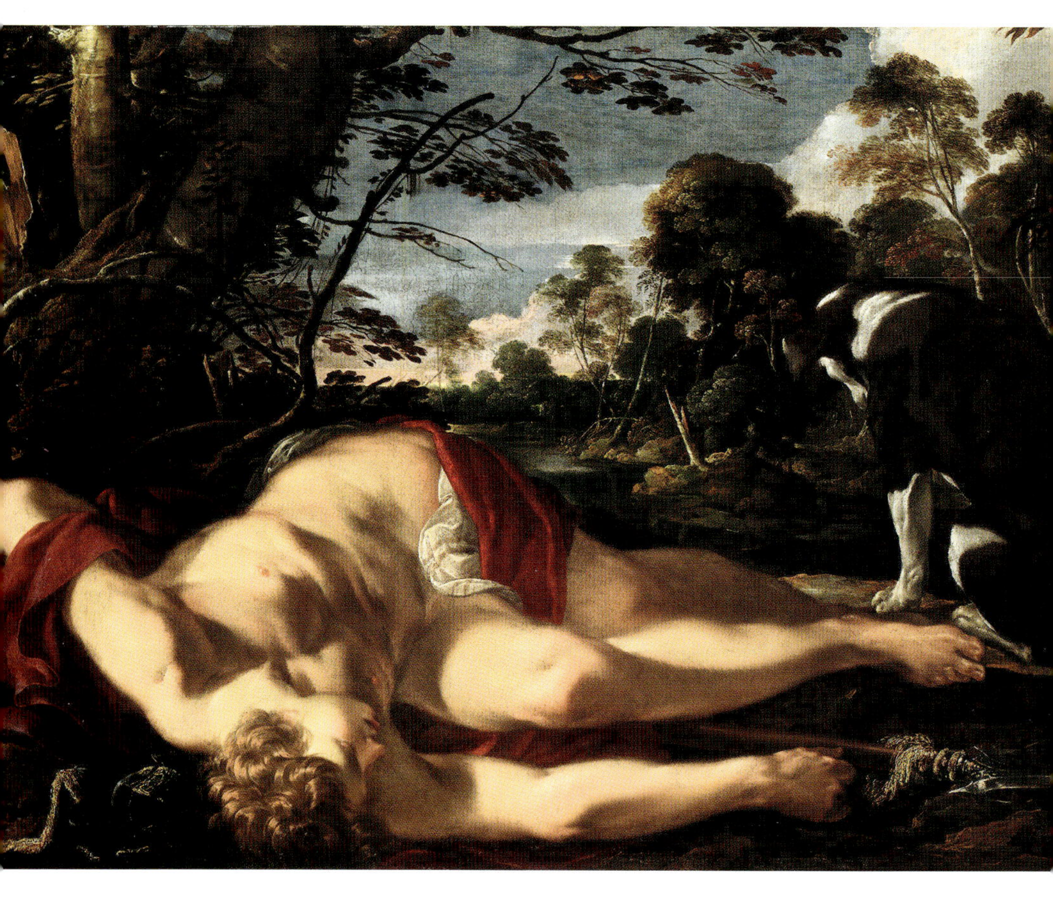

CHAPTER 13
THE SLAYING OF BEAUTY

MEANS · MOTIVE · OPPORTUNITY

Laurent de La Hyre, *Dead Adonis*, about 1624–28
H: 109 cm; L: 148 cm

Second floor, Richelieu, Louis XIII painters, Room 12

Greek Mythology is full of love and crimes. Sometimes these two themes fuse with lust, jealousy and strong passions being not only components of many Greek myths, but also the most common motives for murder. Motives are the causes that move people to induce a certain illegal action, in our case(s) murder. And when immortal gods harbour the feelings described above, it is always easy to find the means, the tools necessary to commit a crime. And it is usually mortals who pay the price.

We enter the painting through the subtle cry of the mourning dog. We might not know his name, he may not be as famous as Argos, the dog of Ulysses, but he is as loyal, remaining beside his dead master's body. But who is this dead man, whose classical beauty will soon fade, swept away by death's touch? His name is Adonis and the myth around him was a great source of inspiration for 17th-century artists.[1]

He was the son of an illegitimate and incestuous love, brought upon a young maiden from the curse of a goddess. Smyrna (otherwise known as Myrrha) was a young woman without any loving or sexual desires. Aphrodite[2] the goddess of love and

---

1. Stéphane Loire, "Adonis mort, un nouveau tableau de Laurent de la Hyre (1606–1656) au Musée du Louvre", *Études, Revue du Louvre*, 3: 1998, pp. 46–55.

2. A.k.a. Venus in Roman mythology.

sexuality was furious when she learnt of this: how could a human deny her gifts? As revenge, she put a spell on Smyrna to fall in love with her own father, Cinyras. And so she did.

Her body started burning with desire for her parent and she satisfied her incestuous lust with a devious ruse. Dressed as a maid, she snuck into her father's bedroom, seduced him and satisfied her sexual craving. As a result, she became pregnant with her own father's child.

When Cinyras discovered the truth, he decided to kill his daughter in order to wash away his family's shame. After a frantic chase, he caught her and just as he was about to strike her with his sword, Aphrodite intervened. Regretting her curse on Smyrna, Aphrodite turned the young woman into a tree (since known as a Myrrh tree). So, when her father's sword cut her in half a baby was born from her trunk.

This was no ordinary baby. He was the most beautiful creature the world has ever seen. His name was Adonis. Aphrodite who was overlooking the scene fell instantly in love with him.

His face and muscular lean body that now lies lifeless in the painting, along with his grace and radiance, made the name Adonis synonymous with male beauty. Before his tragic ending, he was Aphrodite's young protégé, the object of her desire, her lover and her most precious belonging. She was enchanted by this man who was born out of her own enchantments. Yet this love story would cause her pain from loss, a feeling she had never experienced before.

Ares[1] the god of War was renowned for his violent character. He grew jealous of Aphrodite's love for Adonis. How could

1. A.k.a. Mars in Roman mythology.

a mortal be the subject of the beautiful goddess's love, when he – a god – was rejected by her? So when Adonis went hunting in the forests of Cyprus, where he lived with Aphrodite, Ares found the perfect opportunity, the perfect chance to follow through on his murderous intention. He turned himself into a wild boar and attacked the young man. Neither his spear, laying useless under his dead body, nor Aphrodite's love could save him.

Here, we are witnessing the scene moments after the murder of Adonis. The wild boar is nowhere in sight. The scarlet tunic covering his body becomes a river of blood[1] as it meets the earth. The young man's life – his past, his present and his future – is represented in the painting as we look from left to right.

On the far left we see his mother, the cut Myrrh tree trunk that gave birth to him, shedding perfumed tears over her son's corpse.

Then we move to his dead body, whose beauty will soon vanish. And after death, a new circle of life will begin. Maybe his dog, with his back to us is looking at his master's new form, as it grows from the ground. From his blood, Aphrodite will create the red rose, a symbol of love and lust forever after.

And from Aphrodite's tears – she who had never until then or since then shed them – another flower will be born: the anemone, which with its fragile purple petals, blown by the winds, will live as briefly as Adonis did.

1. Vincent Pomarède, Anja Grebe, *Le Louvre: toutes les Peintures*, Skira Flammarion, 2012, p. 523.

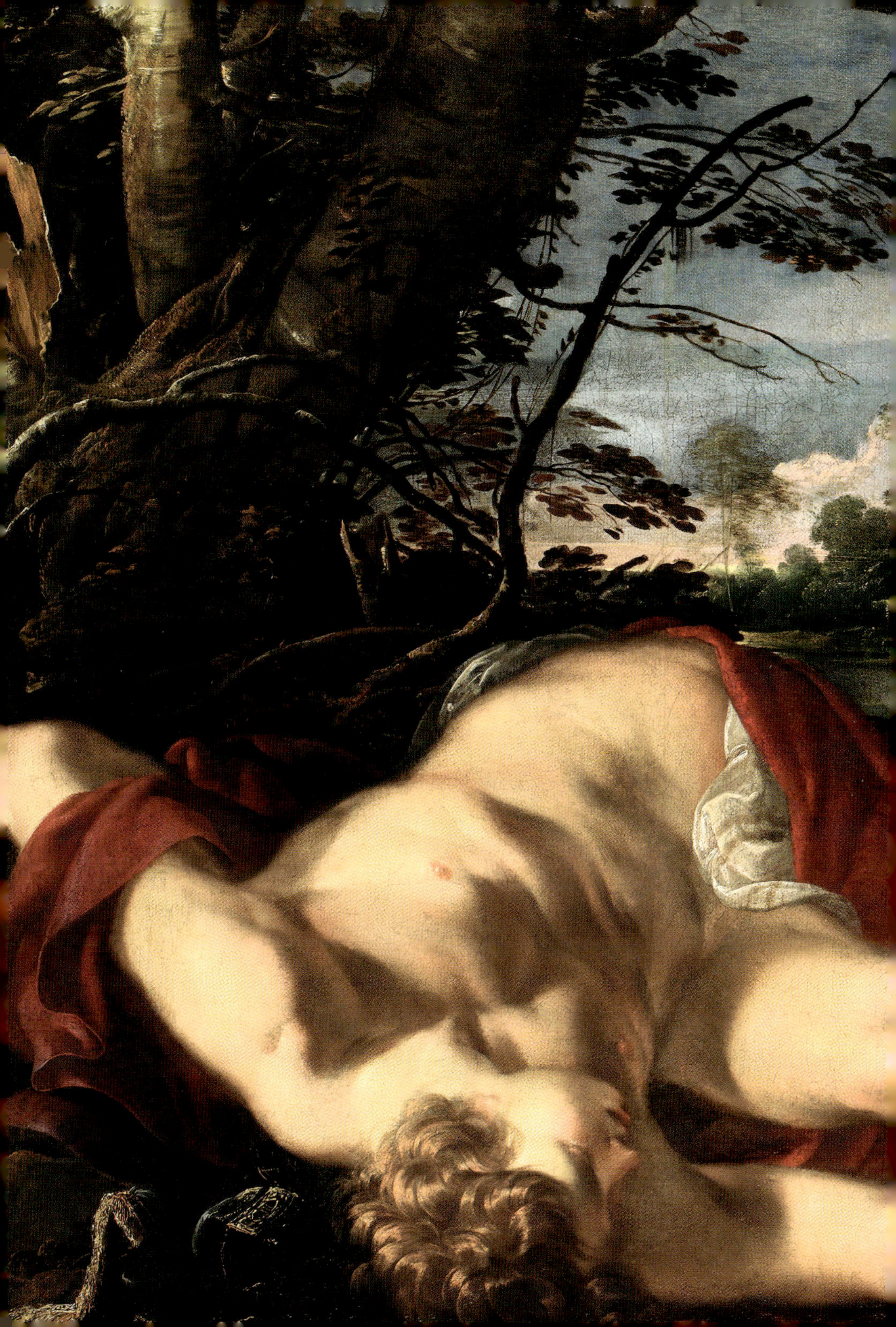

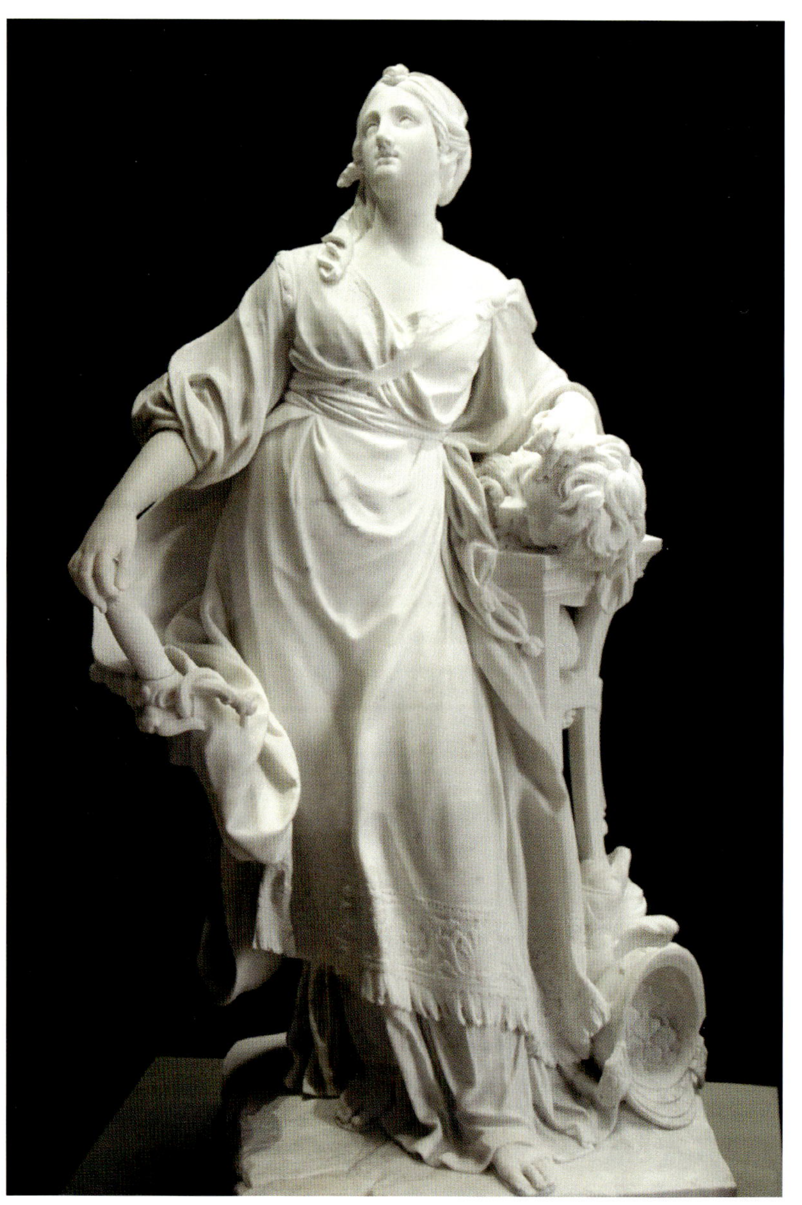

CHAPTER 14
THE SEDUCER WITH THE SWORD

WOMEN WHO KILL - HEROIC MURDERESS

François Ladatte, *Judith with the Head of Holofernes*, 1736
Marble, H: 90 cm; L: 53 cm; D: 35 cm

Ground Floor, Richelieu, Sculptures,
Small Academy Gallery, Room 25, Display case 1

Murders committed by women have always fascinated us. They have also been a challenging subject for religions, arts and sciences. A woman who takes a life was considered until recently almost unnatural, as women are the givers of life, not the ones to take it. A female that kills was seen as a moral and natural monster. She was depicted as a witch, a poisoner, a barbarian, a vamp, a femme fatale!

Frozen in a moment in time, in her most glorious act we see Judith, whose story has served as inspiration for many artists throughout the ages, from Caravaggio to Michelangelo, from Mantegna to Klimt. Her head stretches out from her low-neck dress, her face towards God, giving Him thanks for the strength He gave her to kill her people's enemy, Holofernes.[1]

His severed head – which was prey to her beauty and visible sexual appeal – is resting on a column under her elbow; her body is leaning towards it. Her one hand is touching his hair, ever so gently as if caressing it. In her other hand she holds his sword, which served her as a weapon. By the size

1. Book of Judith, the Old Testament.

of its grip, we can see it is too large for her delicate hands, too heavy for this woman to handle. And yet she did, with God's help.

Her story derives from the Bible. The Assyrian King, Nebuchadnezzar, sent his most successful general, Holofernes, to conquer the world. The people who resisted him vanished. Those who surrendered were enslaved.

The Jews were besieged within the town of Bethulia. After thirty-four days of siege, suffering from famine and lack of water, all hope was lost. They considered surrendering. Then Judith, a young and strikingly beautiful widow, called the elders into her house and told them not to give up the city. She would save them all, with God by her side.

She prayed and prepared for her mission. She brushed her hair and tied a ribbon around it. She then put on her best dress and her finest jewellery and perfumed her body. She would charm anyone who would lay eyes on her.

Accompanied by her loyal slave she left the city en route to the Assyrian camp. When she arrived she spread the word to her enemies that she held the secret to conquering Bethulia without any losses. Her ruse had its effects and she was brought before Holofernes. When he saw her, he was blinded by her beauty.

She made it clear that if he listened to her, God would grant him victory, as "the Jews were about to sin". Holofernes agreed, as "she was not only beautiful, but wise too". On the third night of her sojourn at the enemy's camp, the general invited her into his tent, where he was holding a banquet. It would be the occasion to make her his.

His excitement was such that he drank all night. So, by the time everyone but Judith left his tent, he was drunk and fast asleep. This was the moment she had planned for! With two strikes she cut off his head with his own sword, then placed it in a sack and made her way back to her town, holding up the severed head as a trophy. The Jews hung it from a wall of Bethulia, regained their courage, and won over the Assyrians who were terrified by the sight of their dead chief.

Though it is said that women usually kill by poison, this is more of a perception than a reality. It wasn't the method of choice in Judith's story, nor is it much used nowadays. According to the FBI Supplemental Homicide Report of 1999–2012, women in the United States kill mostly with a gun (39%), a knife (23%), by beating (12%) or by other means (12%), while only a small percentage (2.5%) use poison. Furthermore, killings committed by women are more likely to be in self-defence. They rarely kill strangers. Their victims are usually abusive family members or companions.

Far from common, Judith is acting as a defence shield for her people. She is the hand of divine justice. Judith is the archetype of the heroic murderess. She kills to save her city and knows that she will be honoured for it. By killing a stranger, however, an enemy with whom she had no personal involvement, her act doesn't have the tragic element that we witness in some of the murders committed by other female hands within the museum.

She doesn't face the torment of Medea who kills what she loves the most (see chapter "Searching for the Truth"); she hasn't suffered like Thomyris who kills in order to avenge her son's treacherous death (see chapter "A Mother's Revenge").

And lastly, unlike Charlotte Corday who commits murder knowing that it will cost her life (see chapter "The invisible Murderess"), Judith knows that she will be glorified by her people for this act.

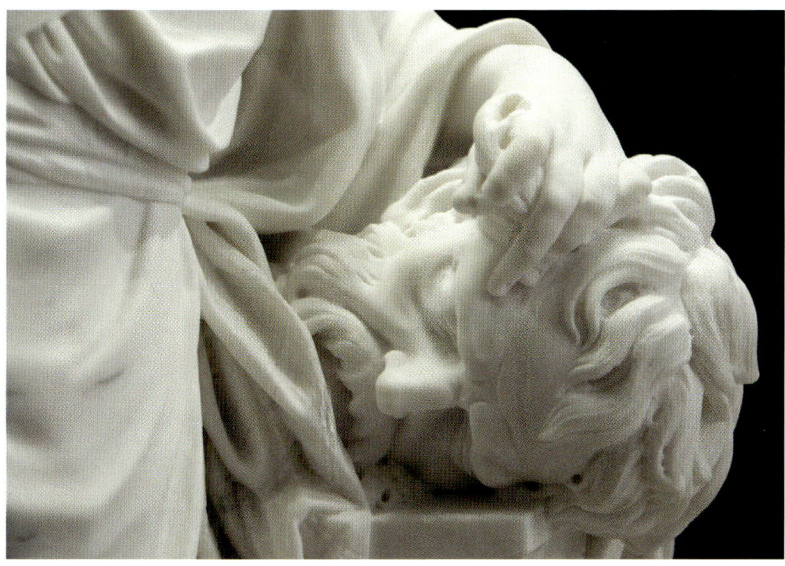

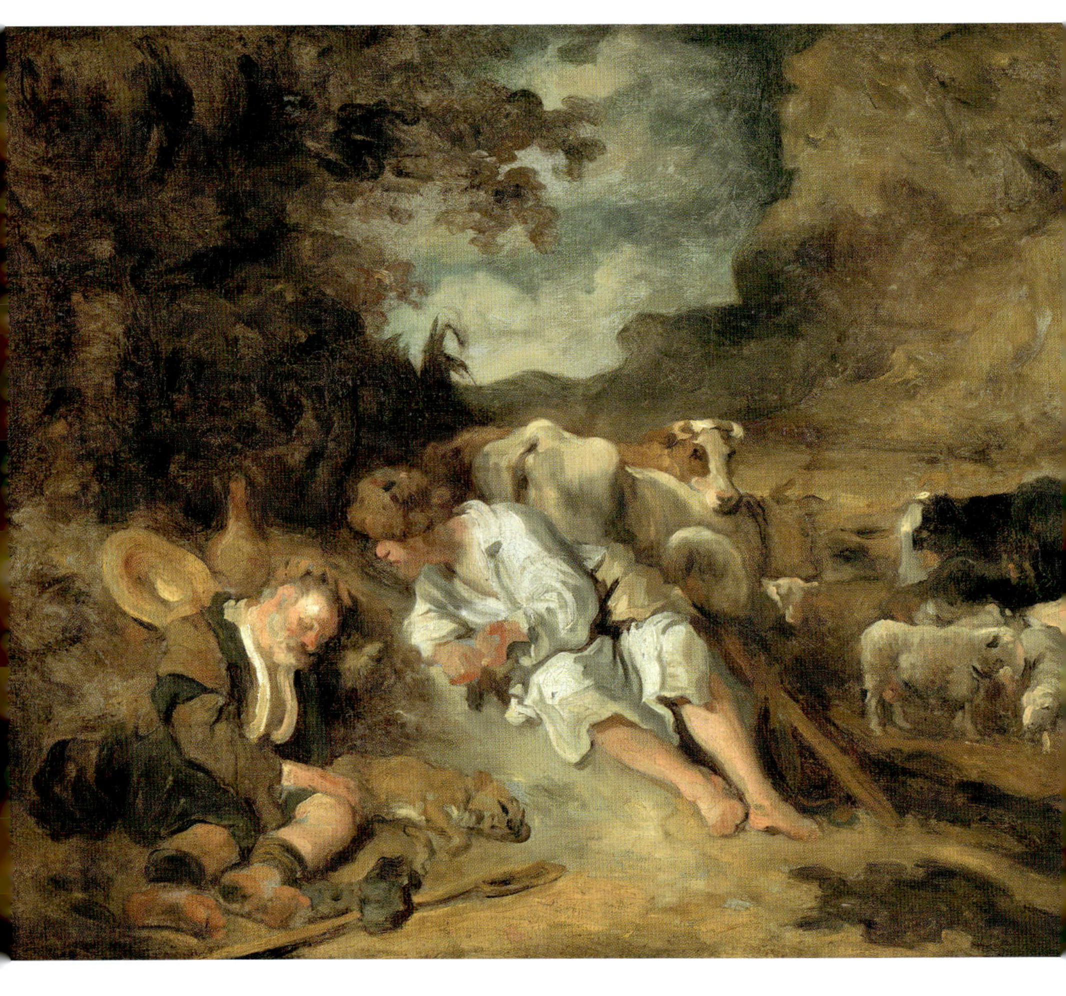

CHAPTER 15
A HUNDRED EYES FOREVER SHUT

TERATOCIDE

Jean-Honoré Fragonard, *Mercury Preparing to Kill the Giant Argus in order to Free the Nymph Io, who Has Been Transformed into a Cow*, about 1761–62
copy of a painting by the Dutch painter Carel Fabritius (1622–1654)
in the Los Angeles County Museum of Art
H: 59 cm; L: 73 cm

Second floor, Sully, Jean-Honoré Fragonard, Room 48

In the times when the twelve Olympian gods ruled the world, becoming the object of their wrath or desire usually ended badly. This also applied to third parties, who ended up dead as collateral damage. We are about to witness this in the painting before us.

Everything looks peaceful and calm in this bucolic country scene. There are cows and sheep in the background. A shepherd with his dog lying next to him is sleeping under a tree in the middle of the day. Nothing prepares us for what is about to happen. Except perhaps the posture of the second man, dressed as a shepherd too, and leaning over the old man.

Nothing is as it seems and no one is who we think they are. We are seconds away from a premeditated, cold-blooded murder. The sleeping shepherd is in fact a monster with 100 eyes. His name is Argus the Panoptes (Πανόπτης, *Greek, for he who sees it all*). He is always awake, resting only 50 of his eyes at a time. The goddess Hera has employed him as a guard. His duty is to prevent one of her husband Zeus' mistresses from escaping. The name of this mistress is Io and we can see her in the painting, though not in human form.

Previously, Io was a young and beautiful priestess in Hera's temple in Argos.[1] When Zeus saw her, he lusted after her. To make her his, he had to devise a plan to seduce Io without his wife knowing. So he turned her into a heifer. He then covered Earth with a thick cloud, to ensure that nothing would be seen from the skies where his wife lived, and mated with Io. In this painting, Io is the white cow we see in the middle, with the back of her body towards us.

When mortals protested to Hera about the thick cloud that covered the sun resulting in their crops dying, she realized that something was wrong. She knew her husband far too well and it didn't take her long to understand that he was cheating on her again. She blew the cloud away and caught him caressing Io's shiny white cow skin.

When she asked him what he was doing, Zeus calmly told her he was just admiring this beautiful animal. But Hera was no fool. She asked for the cow as a gift, as a proof of love. Zeus could not refuse. Hera took her husband's mistress, tied her to an olive tree and had the forever-awake Argus guard her against escape or rescue. And yet in Fragonard's painting (a copy of a Carel Fabritius' work)[2] Argus has fallen asleep.

But who is this man, shadowing over him like death? He is no man. He is the god Hermes,[3] the messenger of the gods. And he is on a mission from Zeus to kill Argus and free his mistress.

---

1. Argos is an ancient Greek city in the Peloponnese.
2. Carel Fabritius, *Mercury and Argus*, 1693, The Los Angeles County Museum of Art.
3. Mercury in Roman mythology.

Disguised as a shepherd, he approached Argus and started talking to him, boring him with his stories. But that was not enough to shut all of his 100 eyes. So Hermes played his flute to make Argus fall asleep. Next to the sleeping monster, he is now ensuring that all eyes are shut.[1] We, on the other hand, see but one pair of eyes. Hermes is about to strike and commit Teratocide, the killing of a monster, (from the Greek word Τέρας –*Teras*, meaning monster).

If it were a film, in the next sequences we would see Hermes decapitating Argus, his head falling on the ground and Io being set free. Hera would gather the eyes of Argus one by one and attach them on the tail of a peacock, her favourite bird, as we can see in the following painting, also in the Louvre.

Unlike Argus, Io's life is spared. She is free but her torment isn't over yet. She will wander the world, cursed by the constant sting of a maddening gadfly, sent by Hera. In her laboured travels, she will pass and name the Ionian Sea after herself. She will run through Illyria and Scythia, climb the Caucasus, give the Bosporus its name (Greek Βόσπορος, *meaning the passage of the calf*) and end up in Egypt. There, Zeus will turn her into a woman again and she will give birth to his son, whose name will be Epaphus (meaning he who was conceived by touch).

1. Sophie Raux, "Carel Fabritius Eighteenth-Century Paris", *The Burlington Magazine*, no. 1307, vol. CLIV, February 2012, p. 104.

Io's name was given to one of the planet Zeus' (Jupiter's) satellites. So that after all that she had been through in the name of love, she would stay at her beloved Zeus' side, in the sky.

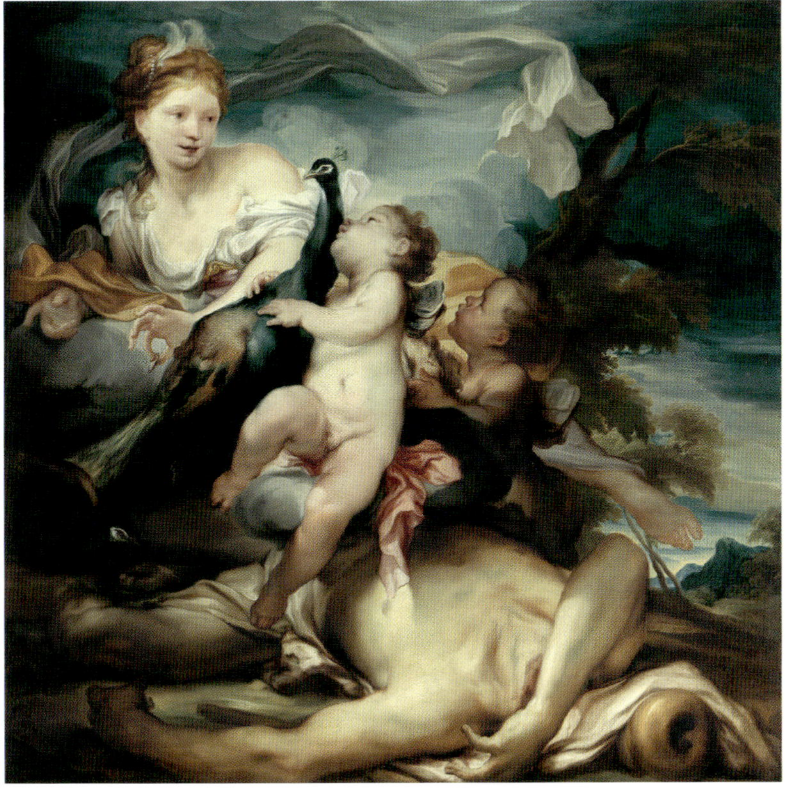

Gregorio de Ferrari, *Junon and Argus*, 1685-1695
Denon, 1st floor, Salvator Rosa, Room 13

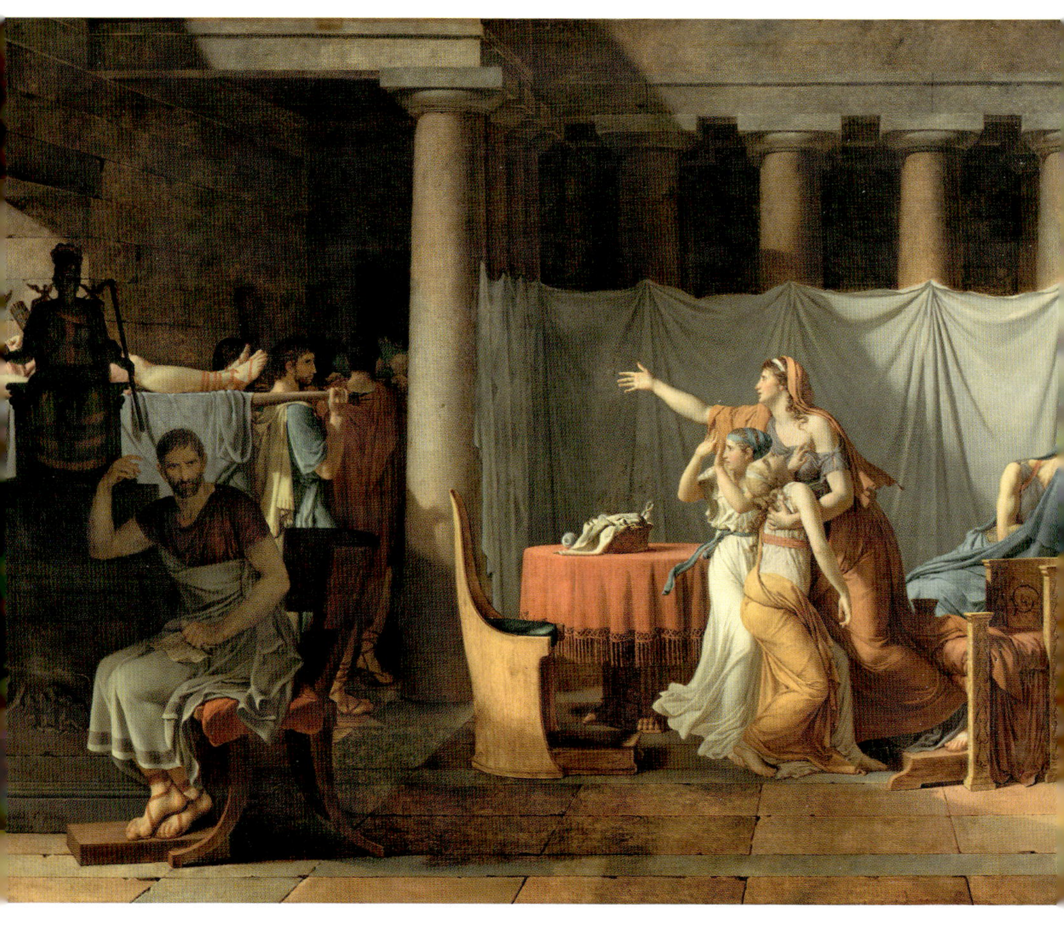

CHAPTER 16
THE STATE ABOVE FAMILY

CAPITAL SENTENCE

Jacques-Louis David,
The Lictors Bring to Brutus the Bodies of His Sons, 1789
H: 323 cm; L: 422 cm

First Floor, Denon, Daru, Room 75

The act of taking one's life is not only committed by individuals. State power can also inflict death upon people, based on law. Capital Punishment otherwise known as the death penalty can be imposed as a lawful sentence by the State. Although two-thirds of the world's countries have abolished or ceased to apply the death penalty,[1] it still remains applicable in certain US states and in China among other countries. Its adversaries consider the death sentence to be murder committed by the State. So whether justified, lawful or otherwise, as a form of killing it finds a place in this book.

The Lictors Bring, to Brutus, the Bodies of His Sons takes us back, once more, to troubled Roman times in the late 6th century BC. Only this time, a father finds himself in the middle of a conflict of interests.

The tableau is divided into three parts. On the lower right side, a group of four women are expressing their grief with horror and shock.[2] Three of them avoid facing the funeral cortege, in the background on the left. One covers her face under a veil, another faints in her mother's arms and the third shields

---

1. http://www.worldcoalition.org/moratorium.html
2. Thomas Kirchner, *Les Reines de Perse aux pieds d'Alexandre de Charles le Brun: Tableau-manifeste de l'art Français du XVIIe siècle*, Editions de la Maison des Sciences de l'Homme, 2013.

her eyes with both hands. Only one woman watches the procession in desperation. She is the mother of the young girls. She is also the mother of the two dead men brought to their house by the Lictors.[1]

The body of the second son arrives after the first, which has already been carried deeper into the family house. Their names are Titus and Tiberius. They were executed for high treason, under the orders of the man who is seated on the lower left, calm, engaging us with an authoritative stare. His name is Lucius Junius Brutus.[2] He is the founder of the Roman Republic. He is also the dead men's father.

Brutus was raised in the house of his uncle Lucius Tarquinius Superbus, who was to be Rome's last king. Brutus' father and brothers were considered threats to Tarquinius' reign and consequently were murdered by the king. Brutus was spared because he was thought to be an imbecile.[3] Yet this was his ruse so he could plan revenge on his family's death without being noticed.

An opportunity presented itself when a noble woman, by the name of Lucretia, was raped by the King's son, Sextus Tarquinius. Despite a public outrage Sextus remained unpunished and subsequently Lucretia committed suicide. Brutus, with the support of the people and the army sent the king and his family into exile. He established democracy, gave birth to the Roman Republic and became one of its Consuls, the highest elected political office. He also demanded that the

1. Lictors were Roman civil servants, bodyguards to magistrates who held the right to command.

2. *Not* the same person as Brutus who killed Julius Cesar.

3. Brutus in Latin means stupid.

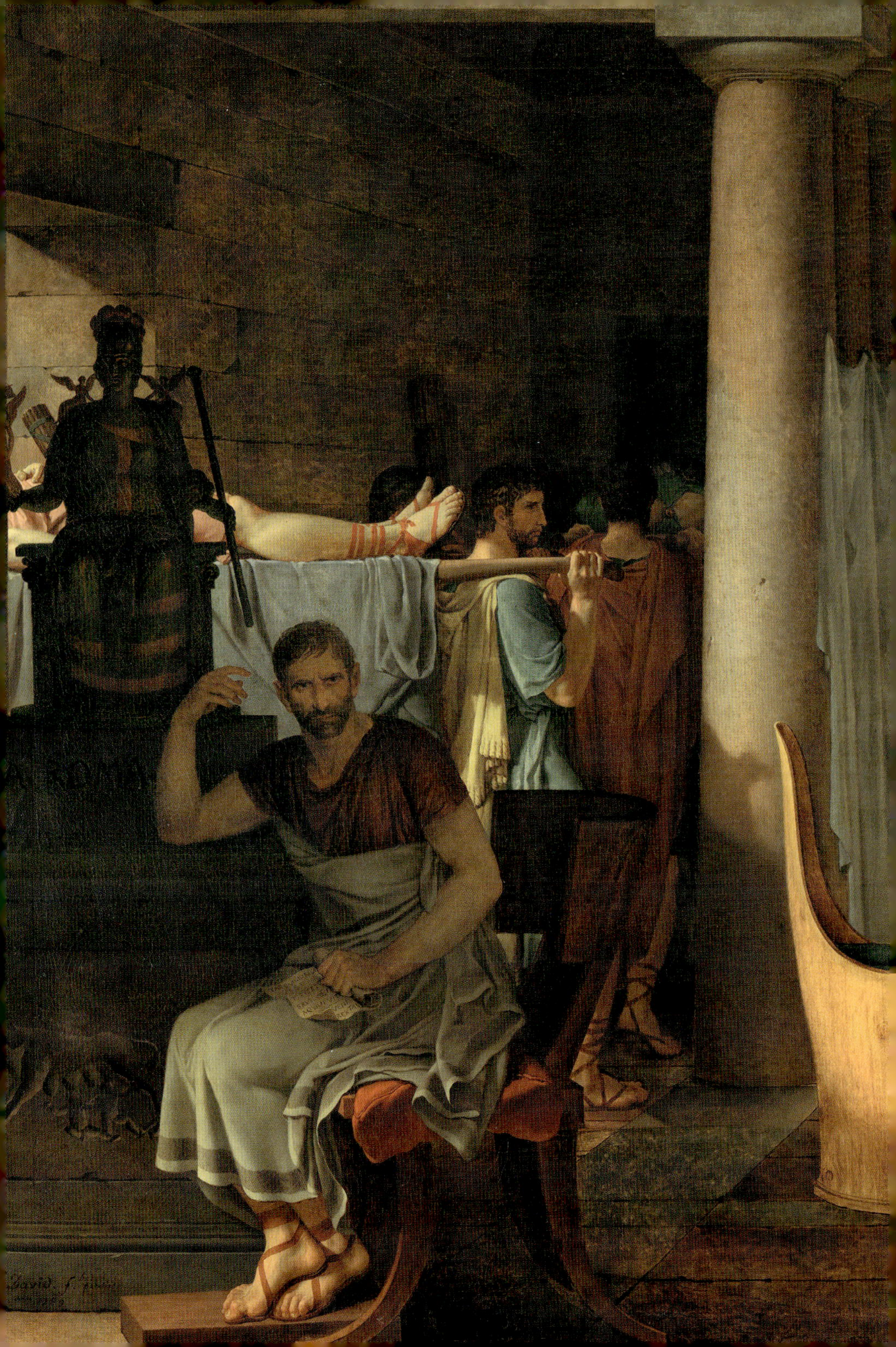

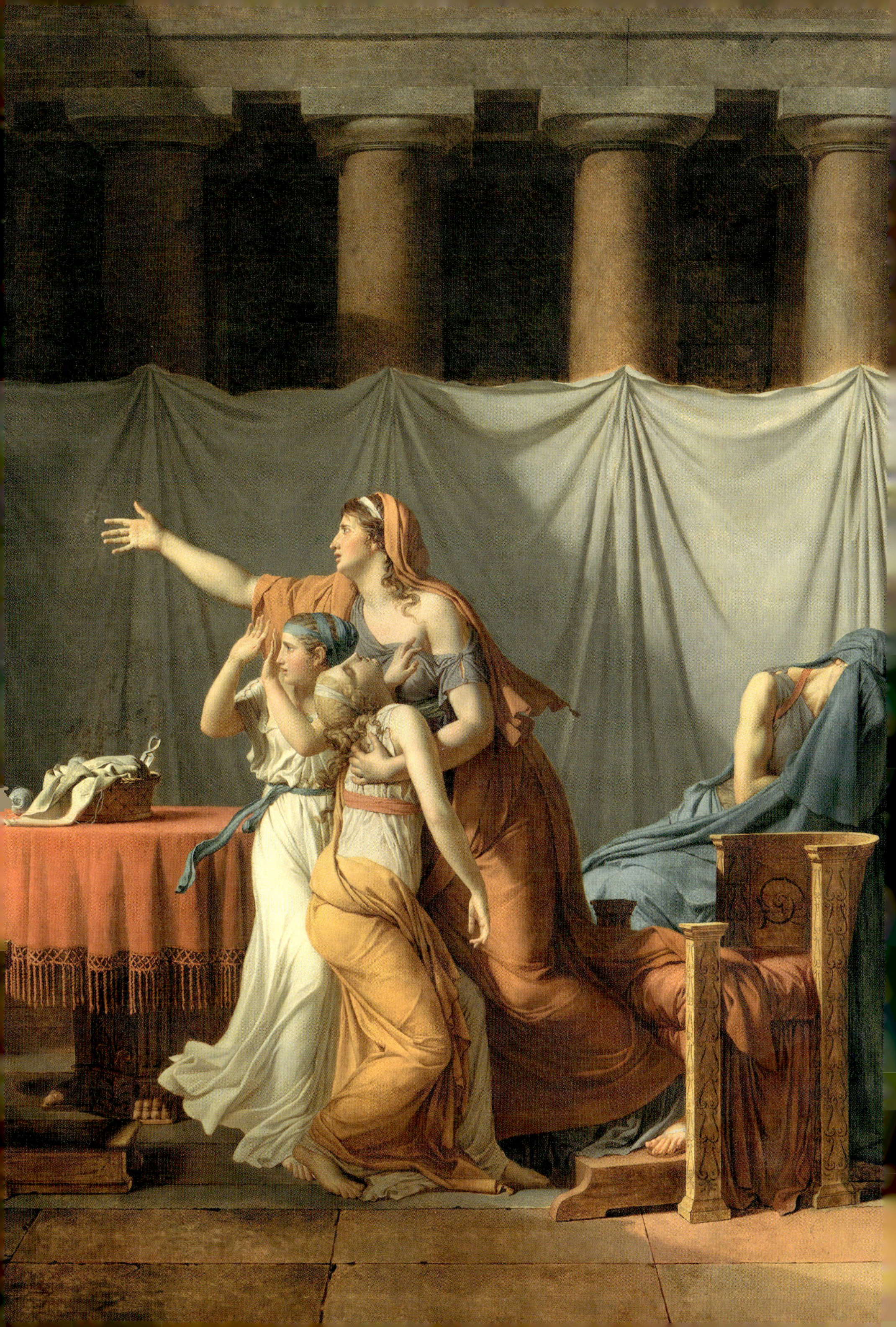

population take an oath to never again allow any man to become king.[1]

During Brutus' rule the exiled Tarquinii family tried to regain the throne, by conspiring with powerful Roman citizens. Among the conspirators were Brutus' two sons! When their plot was exposed, Brutus took action. As a consul he was bound by his position to punish the traitors. Even if that meant putting to death his offspring.

The scene before us is taking place just after their execution. Mother and sisters are mourning, while Brutus shows no sign of emotion. But in the intensity of his tight grip around his sons' death warrant and his clenched feet we can read his paternal grief.[2]

Above Brutus stands a statue representing Rome, signifying that the interest of the Roman Republic is of higher importance than a father's role.

There is yet another layer to this tableau, one that reveals its creator's political views.[3] Painted by Jacques-Louis David, in 1789, the year of the French revolution, it manifests the painter's Republican beliefs and antiroyalist sentiments.[4]

An ancient Roman subject serves as an analogy to a contemporary political issue. In this case the painter considered that royalty was "*dépassée*". Louis XVI and Marie Antoinette,

---

1. Cassius Dio, *Roman History*, Books 2-3.
2. William Eisler, "A Father's Tears: The Image of Brutus in the Dassiers' Medallic History of the Roman Republic", *The Burlington Magazine*, CL, March 2008.
3. Claire Maingon, *Le Salon et ses artistes. Histoire des expositions du Roi Soleil aux Arts Français*, Paris: Hermann Editions, 2009, p. 64.
4. Blandine Chavanne, Exh. cat., *Libertés et contraintes, la peinture comme modèle pour la tragédie. Le Théâtre des Passions 1697–1759*, Musée de Beaux-Arts de Nantes, Editions Fage, 2011.

as the Tarquinii family, are doing harm to their subjects, so they must go. For David, being a good citizen is more important than being a good father: democracy is the ideal and in order to establish a Republic you need to shed blood. Even if it's that of your own family.

And this would become the axiom of the most radical French Revolutionary group that between 1793 and 1794 would drown France in blood, in order to impose their political ideas.[1]

1. Philippe Bodres, *Autour de Brutus de David: commentaires anciens et modernes*, Scenna Editions, 2001.

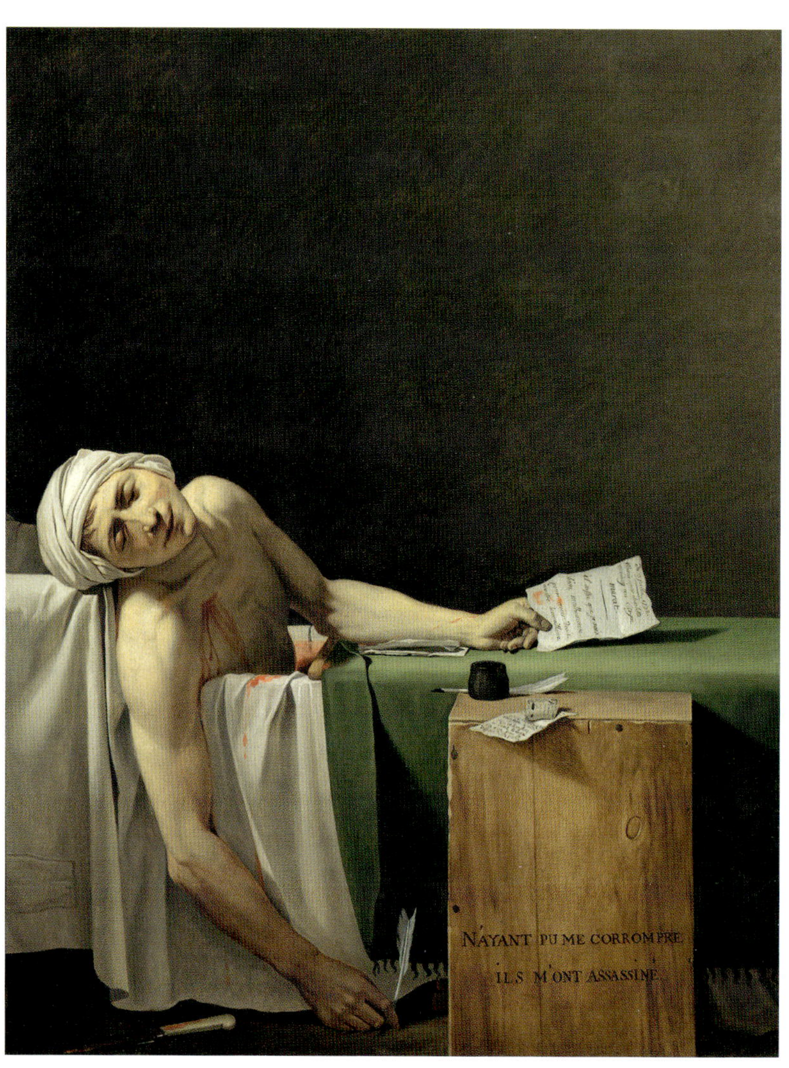
N'AYANT PU ME CORROMPRE
ILS M'ONT ASSASSINÉ

CHAPTER 17

THE INVISIBLE MURDERESS

ASSASSINATION · WOMEN WHO KILL · CRIME SCENE

Jacques-Louis David (studio replica),
The Death of Marat, 1794
H: 162 cm; L: 130 cm

Second floor, Sully,
David and his students: the art of portrait, Room 54

A work of art is not only the concrete expression of its creator's imagination and talent. It can also express an artist's religious, philosophical or social beliefs, political ideology or worldview in general.

This painting is one of the most famous French works, and perhaps the most well-known depiction of a revolutionary event: the assassination of Marat. Assassination is the murder of a prominent person, usually a politician, political leader or ruler, commonly for political reasons.

This work, which is a contemporary copy of the original by the artist's studio[1], serves as a sound example of art as an ideological, even propaganda medium.[2] This is achieved not only by what it actually shows, but in this case, by what it doesn't show.

Marat was, along with Robespierre, one of the Revolutionary regime's most prominent and powerful men. His newspaper *l'Ami du peuple* (The Friend of the People) was the voice of the French Revolution's most extreme party, the very same group that had led the country into the reign of Terror. During this

---

1. The original work is in the Royal Museum of Beaux Arts in Brussels.

2. Exh. cat., *The Repeating Image: Multiples in French Painting from David to Matisse*, 7 October 2007 – 1 January 2008. Baltimore: The Walters Art Museum, 2007, p. 25.

period, between the years 1793 and 1794, political adversaries, members of the clergy or nobility or anyone who posed a possible threat, were guillotined by the hundreds. The most moderate Revolutionary group, the Girondins – had thus suffered great losses.

Within the milieu of the Girondins, Charlotte Corday a twenty-five-year-old woman from Caen, a city in Normandy, witnessed France drowning in its citizens' own blood, at the hands and ideology of the Montagnards.

Something had to be done and she believed she was the one to do it. Her plan was to kill the main representative of these political extremists, Jean-Paul Marat. She made her way to Paris and looked for him at the Senate. However, that day, his skin disease had kept him at home, where he was soothing his eczema in a bathtub filled with mint water. Claiming she was in possession of a list of Girondins from Caen, Corday gained entry into his home. Marat promised that he would have the people on the list brought to Paris and decapitated by the next morning.

She grabbed the knife that she had bought the same morning and hidden in her bosom, and stabbed him in the chest. He was dead within minutes. It was the 13th of July 1793.

This painting captures the moment when Marat's last breath leaves his body. You are standing in front of an actual crime scene. Only the message "DO NOT CROSS – CRIME SCENE" written on plastic yellow tape is missing, along with CSI personnel and their suitcase equipped with forensic tools.

But most significantly there is a person missing from this painting: the murderess. And yet without a doubt, the woman who had just killed Marat is standing next to her victim, waiting for his supporters to arrest her. Her absence is not accidental. It serves not only an artistic purpose but, more importantly, an ideological one.

The painter, David, was an advocate of the radical Revolutionary forces and a personal friend of Marat. He was one of the last people to have seen him alive, just the previous day, in the same bathtub, writing his explosive words against his political adversaries. So when he offered to paint his death portrait, he knew exactly how to represent him.

We are introduced to him by the quote featured on the wooden trunk that served him as a desk. It reads: "Having not been able to corrupt me, they killed me", suggesting the motive – according to the artist – behind this crime[1]. And from that we move up to the pale, luminous flawless figure. There are no signs of the skin disease, only a calm face, bathed in a soft light.

In one hand he holds Corday's letter, in the other his plume. His idealized features, his wound and most importantly his posture, along with his hand hanging lifeless on the side brings to mind a Pieta,[2] even though the female element is absent. Marat is not just another dead politician. He is a Christ figure;[3] he is a martyr of the Revolution who sacrificed himself for the good of the people.[4] Thus, in this iconographic depiction the murderer has no place.

1. The original painting, now in the Royal Museum of Beaux Arts in Brussels, has a different quote. It reads: "To Marat. David".

2. A sculpture, painting or drawing of the Dead Christ, supported by the Virgin Mary.

3. Jorg Traeger, *Der Tod des Marat: Revolution des menschenbildes*, Munich: Prestel, 1986.

4. Sébastien Allard, "Marat assassiné, La recherche de l'idéal", in *Portraits Publics – Portraits privés, 1740–1830*, Paris: RMN, 2007, p. 244.

David believes this woman is unworthy of acknowledgement. She will be soon forgotten and no one will remember the name of the pawn of Marat's political enemies who killed the "Friend of the People".

But he was wrong in every aspect. During her brief trial, which ultimately led her to the execution scaffold four days after the assassination, it was proved that she was acting alone. "I have killed one man to save a hundred thousand", she claimed.

In any case the shock of the assassination by a woman's hand was significant. Up until recently a female who kills was considered an unnatural phenomenon. Women are meant to give life, not take it. Furthermore, the knife was not a weapon used by women, as poison was believed to be their preferred option. This is the reason why, according to legend, Charlotte Corday was given a physiological examination when she was arrested; to verify if she was a woman or a man disguised as a woman. Such was the disbelief that a woman could perform such a violent act.

Contrary to David's prediction, Corday was not forgotten. The physical presence he denied her in this painting, was given to her by many other artists. And they often depicted her not as an assassin but rather as an angel of death, as a vamp, as a heroine who sacrificed herself for the good of her country[1] (as seen for example in the following paintings).

1. Jean-Paul Chimot, "Le Marat de David et la Charlotte Corday de Baudry", in *À travers l'art français du Moyen Age au XXe siècle*, Paris: F. De Nobele, 1978, pp. 378–79.

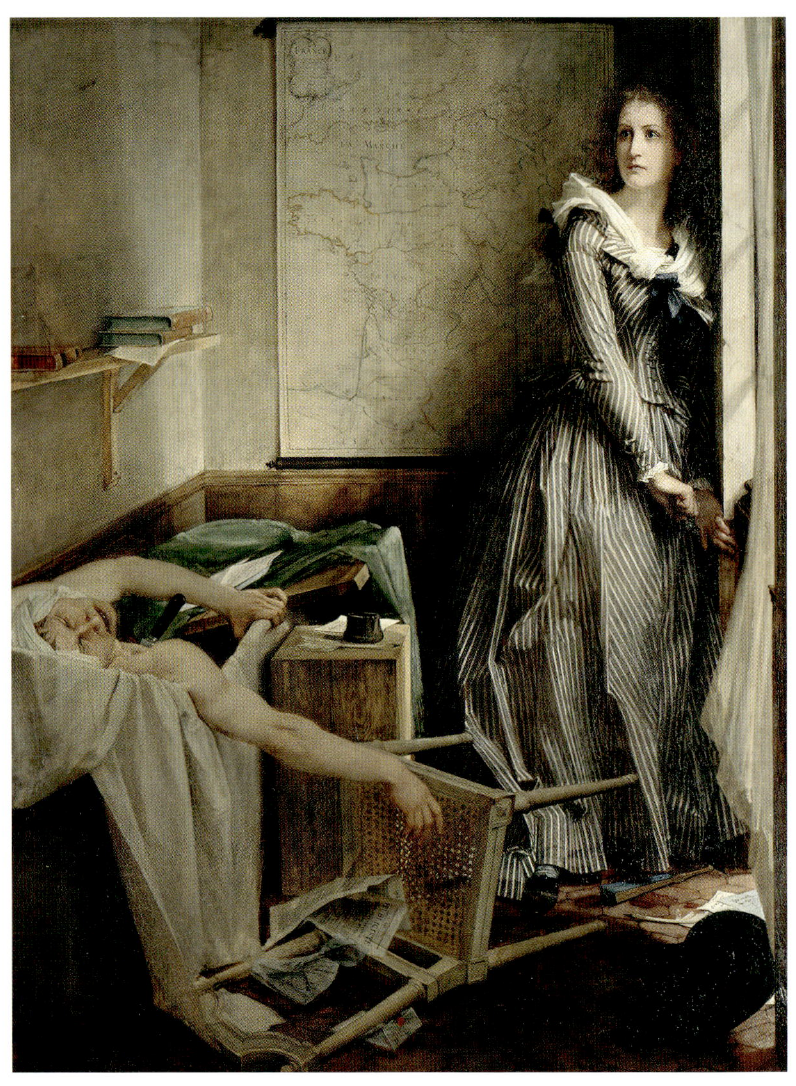

Paul Baudry, *Charlotte Corday*, 1860, The Museum of Art, Nantes

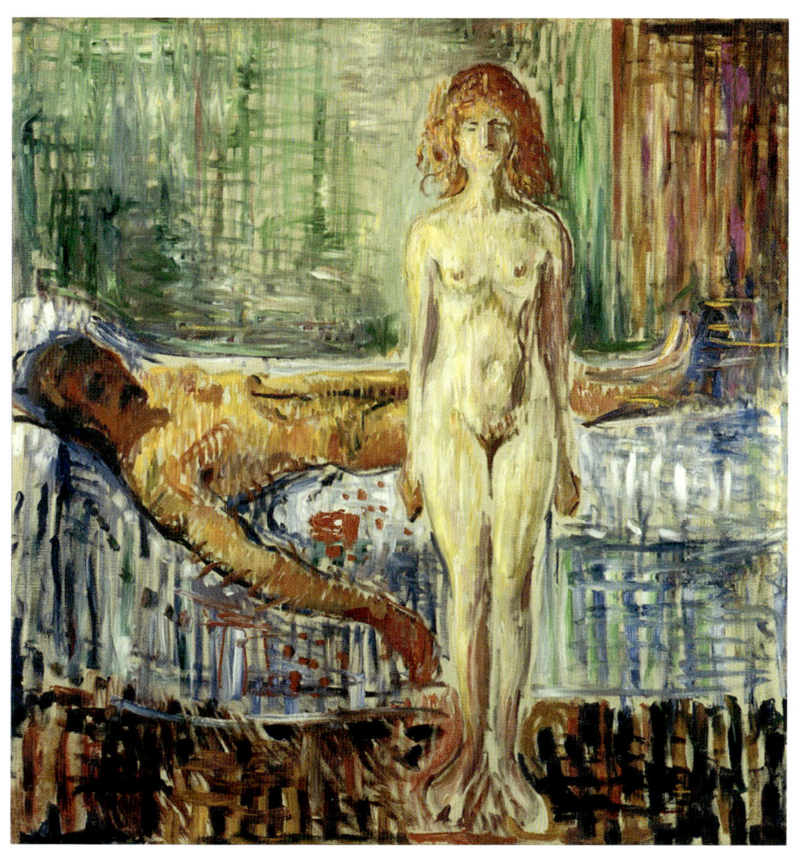

Edvard Munch, *The Death of Marat II*, 1907, Munch Museum, Oslo, Norway

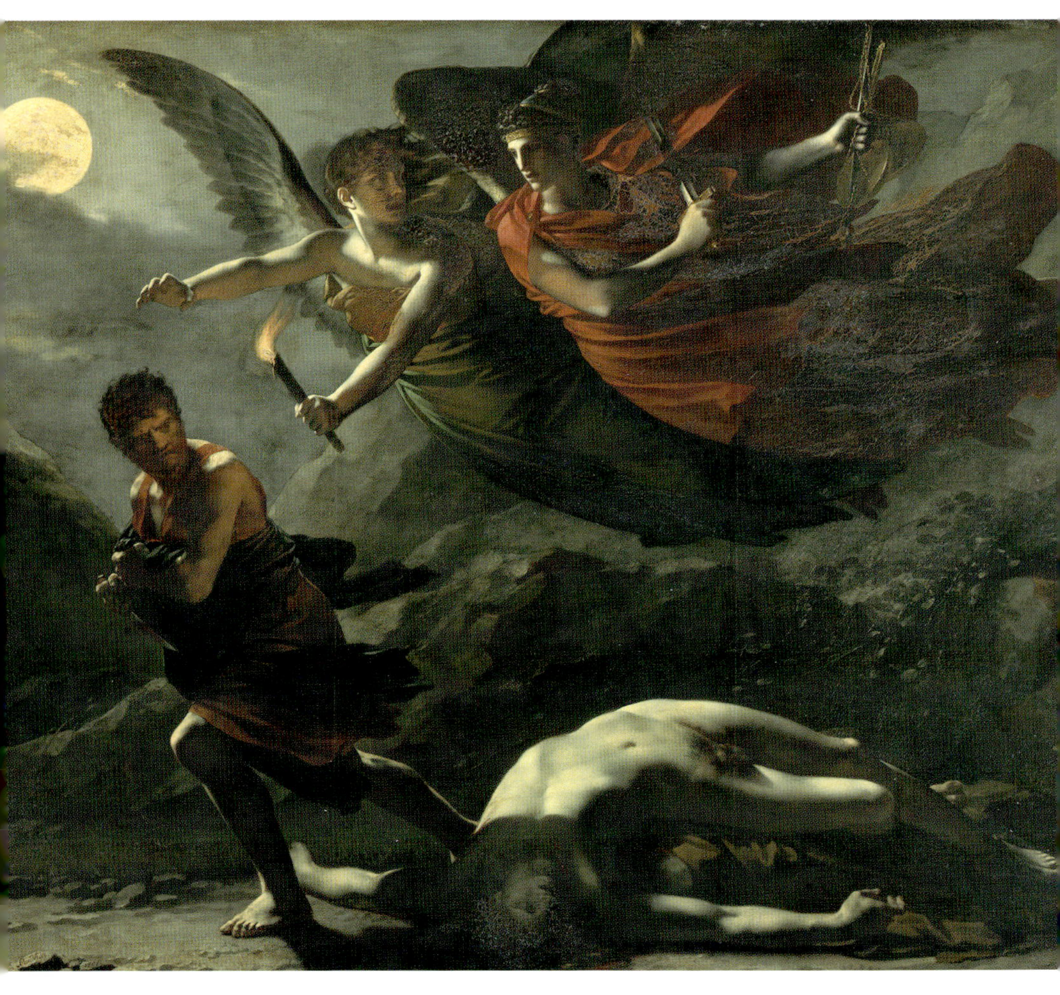

CHAPTER 18
THE EVERLASTING HUNT

JUSTICE - PHYSIOGNOMIC SIGNS - NATURAL-BORN KILLER

Pierre-Paul Prud'hon,
Justice and Divine Vengeance Pursuing Crime, 1808
H: 244 cm; L: 294 cm

First floor, Denon, Daru, Room 75

If the room in the Louvre were empty we would imagine the sound of flapping wings, depicted in this painting. Here, under a harsh light a masterpiece by Prud'Hon is left to degrade. Two centuries ago, during its days of glory, it hung in the Parisian Criminal Court. Reactions to it then were extremely intense.

This is a hunt scene, yet no ordinary one. In the centre of the painting, the lifeless body of a young man lies motionless on the rocks. His transparent pale beauty, reminds us of the Young Martyr (see "Youth under Persecution"). They seem to belong together, forming an ideal couple, united in the eternity of violent death. At the same time, his posture reminds us of the corpses featured in the *Raft of the Medusa* by Gericault (Denon, 1st floor, Room 77), who may have been inspired by Prud'Hon's painting.

On our left, the murderer still holds the knife in his hand. He starts to run, in an attempt to escape with the pouch of money he stole from the victim. As he looks back, throwing a final glance at what he has done, his grotesque face dives into the shadows.[1] The ferocity of his almost primitive characteristics is in stark contrast to the victim's pure, idealized beauty.

---

1. Sylvain Laveissière, Exh. cat., *Prud'Hon, La Justice et la Vengeance divine poursuivant le Crime*, Paris: Editions RMN, 1986.

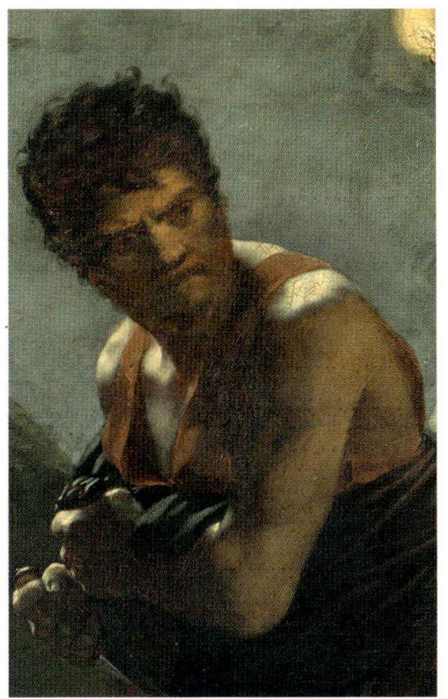

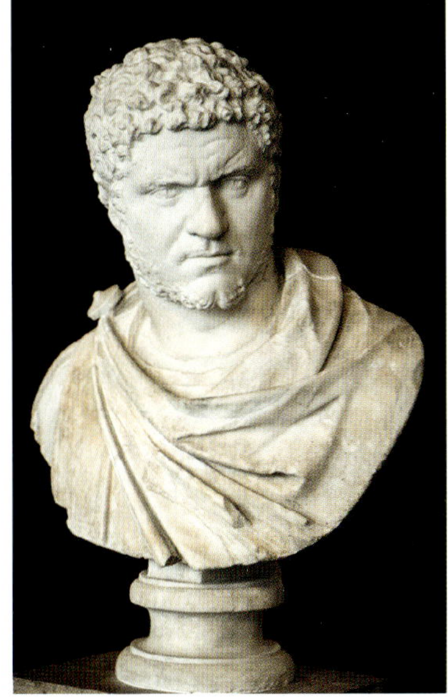

Bust of the Emperor Caracalla,
ground floor, Denon, Roman Antiquities
100 BC–AD 500, room 27

Nothing is more touching than the victim and more dramatically sinister than the criminal's figure.[1]

His looks seem a prescient depiction of the Physiognomic Signs – the Stigmas – that Lombroso, the father of Criminology, attributed to the natural-born killer in the mid-19th century: "The killer's eyes are frosty still, sometimes fiery and bloody. His nose is almost always hooked like a vulture's and always massive. The jaws are big, he has jug ears, pronounced sinuses, protruding chins, and broad cheekbones, his hair is thick and

1. Théophile Gautier, *Guide de l'amateur au Musée du Louvre*, (1867), Paris: Nabu Press, 2013.

black. It's common for his beard to be thin, his bicuspid teeth developed and his lips thin."[1]

Lombroso's profile of a killer – published seventy years *after* the completion of this painting – accurately describes the killer's physique. And yet in front of us we do not have just a man. We have Crime itself. His face resembles that of Caracalla,[2] whose bust[3] Prud'hon likely saw in the same museum. (Ground floor, Denon, Roman Art 3rd–5th centuries AD, Room 27).

In any case, this scene is an allegory of Justice, where no crime is left unpunished. The two winged figures will always be in its pursuit. And they will always prevail. Justice (Themis) and Divine Vengeance (Nemesis) are omnipresent to restore the balance that has been violated by criminal acts.

Justice holds a balance in her hand, the counterweight folded up: the case is already tried; the criminal's guilt is affirmed. Punishment will be imposed on him by the sword she is holding in her other hand. Her body is in motion, yet her hair remains intact, her face is calm, highlighting the composure with which justice is dispensed.

Before her we see Nemesis, Divine Vengeance, holding a torch. She lights Justice's way and the murderer's face, preventing him from disappearing into the shadows. Her hair in a wild dance against the wind, her face mad with fury, she will grab the criminal and deliver him to her partner. The message

1. Cesare Lombroso, *L'uomo delinquent*, 1876.

2. Roman Emperor, 211–17 AD, famous for his brutality. Among others he killed his brother Geta, in order to reign sole over the Roman Empire, and his wife and infant daughter as the former had joined forces with his brother.

3. Prud'hon, *Magazine Pittoresque*, 1838, p. 353.

is clear: no matter how fast criminals run, they'll never escape the reach of these two deities.

The artist's own description of his work reads: "Divine justice is constantly pursuing Crime; it never escapes her. Covered with night's veils, in a remote and wild place, greedy Crime slaughtered his victim. He seized his gold and now looks back to see if there is any sign of life in him, any sign that could lead to his doom. What a fool! He cannot see that Nemesis, Justice's terrible agent, like a vulture after its prey, pursues him. She shall reach him and deliver him to her rigid companion."

This painting, commissioned by a prefect of Paris, replaced the Crucifix in the Criminal Courthouse from 1808 to 1815. Maybe that is why the victim's pose, resembles an inverse crucifixion.

The painting was so powerful, inspiring such total terror,[1] that it's said when criminals entered the Court, they would faint at the sight of it. They knew that it was their very fate being illustrated before them.

1. J.-P. Voïart, *Entretiens sur la théorie de la peinture*, Paris: Alexis Eymery Libraire, 1820.

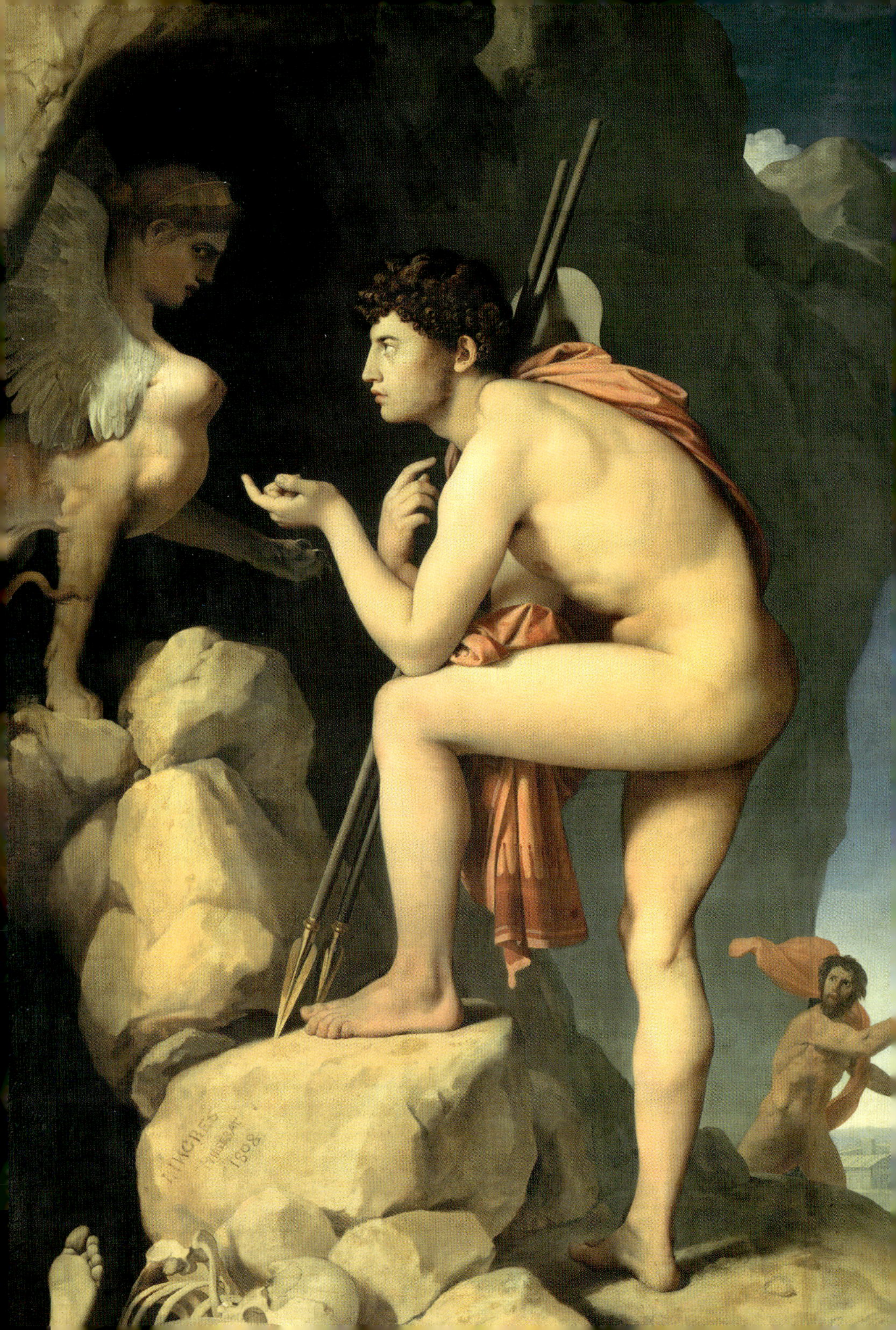
I. INGRES
1808

CHAPTER 19
SON AND HUSBAND. FATHER AND BROTHER. DETECTIVE AND MURDERER

DETECTIVE FICTION · REGICIDE · PATRICIDE

Jean-Auguste-Dominique Ingres,
Oedipus Explaining the Enigma of the Sphinx, 1808
Salon de 1827
H: 189 cm, L: 144 cm

First Floor, Denon, Daru, Room 75

Family matters can prove complicated in ancient Greece. Mythology recounts numerous stories of family members killing each other, even if sometimes they may not even know they are related. The Labdacides family was no exception. Before us, stands the most tragic of all the Greek mythical personages: Oedipus. He is the protagonist of the first Detective Story in the Western world, Sophocles' tragedy "Oedipus Rex", presented to the Athenian public in 428 BC.

A detective-murder-mystery has a highly organized structure and recognized conventions. These include an unresolved murder, a closed circle of suspects with evidence pointing interchangeably to one or another, a private detective or policeman gifted with observation skills and deduction capacities, and the revelation of the killer's identity at the end of the story.[1]

Despite the many suspects, their guilt being based on circumstantial evidence, each one with motive, means and opportunity, the truth is discovered from a logical conclusion based on the clues and details revealed little by little to the reader.[2] All these elements are present in Sophocles' tragedy, classifying it as a true detective story.

---

1. P. D. James, *Talking about Detective Fiction*, Bodleian Library, 2009, p. 15ff.
2. As above.

In Ingres' painting we see Oedipus as a young man facing a winged mythical monster, half lion and half woman, the Sphinx. Earlier he had fled the kingdom of Corinth – the town of which he was a prince and mistakenly considered as his birthplace – in order to avoid a horrible prophecy, which foretold he would kill his father and marry his mother.

Heading towards the city of Thebes,[1] he encounters the Sphinx, a monster superior to man in wisdom and force.[2] She would ask travellers for the answer to her riddle: "*What walks on four feet in the morning, two in the afternoon and three at night*?" When no answer was given or the answer was wrong, she would devour them. The human bones and the foot we see in the painting under her rocky throne are the remains of her victims.

We see a man fleeing the challenge Oedipus is facing. Meanwhile the provocatively feminine[3] monster's paw is ready to strike the young prince down. But Oedipus has the answer to her riddle. "*It is Man: as an infant, he crawls on all fours; as an adult, he walks on two legs and; in old age, he uses a 'walking' stick*". The monster's face turns to anger. Having being defeated for the first time, the Sphinx kills herself, freeing the way to Thebes, which we can see in the lower right corner. Yet Oedipus' intelligence and this correct answer would seal his fate.

1. Thebes was the largest city of the ancient region of Boeotia, leader of the Boeotian confederacy and a major rival of ancient Athens.
2. Exh. cat. *Ingres, In Pursuit of Perfection: The Art of J.A.D Ingres*, P. Condon, M. B. Cohn, A. Mongan, J. B. Speed Art Museum/Kimbell Art Museum, Fort Worth, Texas, 1984, p. 236.
3. Florence Viguier-Dutheil, "À Lens Ingres remplace Delacroix", *Grande Galerie*, Dec. 2013, no. 26, p. 64.

Upon his arrival in Thebes he becomes a hero, the one who killed the monster and saved the city. His reward is the hand in marriage of the recently widowed Queen Jocasta. Her husband, Laius, the king of Thebes, was killed on the outskirts of the city. The murderer is unknown. Oedipus becomes the king and has four children with the queen.

Sophocles' play starts unfolding when Oedipus' new kingdom is struck by plague, the gods' way to show their discontent. According to the oracle the only way to save the city is to find the killer of Laius, the former king, and banish him from the city.

So, the story begins with an unresolved murder. The killer is still at large. Finding him is crucial if the city is to survive. Oedipus as the new king, having already saved the city once before by confronting the Sphinx, takes charge of the investigation. He is our detective.

He starts his interrogation with the prominent men of Thebes. When they offer no leads, the queen's brother Creon intervenes and suggests that he question Tiresias, an old and blind clairvoyant.

The old man refuses to reveal what he knows. This makes Oedipus furious. When the king accuses the blind man of being implicated in his predecessor's murder, the psychic responds by accusing Oedipus himself of foul play.

Oedipus is outraged by these claims. He in turn accuses his wife's brother, Creon, and the old man of killing Laius and now conspiring against him to steal his throne. In his mind, these two are the main suspects. They had the motive, the means and the opportunity to commit the crime, as defined by the conventions of a detective story. Jocasta, the queen, intervenes to temper the situation between her husband and brother.

When she asks for the reason behind the fight, Oedipus quotes the oracle. She urges him not to consider the validity of the prophecies. After all, her husband wasn't killed by his son, as the oracle had foretold, but rather he was believed to have been murdered by bandits on a crossroad, just prior to Oedipus' arrival.

Oedipus then remembers he had killed someone on a crossroad before arriving to Thebes. He asks for a description of the victim, the exact time, the exact place. Shocked, he realizes that he may very well be the killer. But the worst is yet to come. When he discovers from his wife that there is an eyewitness, he calls for him. From that moment, clues start pouring in and the whole story plays out with a terrible twist.

All the answers to the crime are found in Oedipus' past, one that he himself was not aware of. He didn't know that when Laius, the King of Thebes, and his wife Jocasta finally had a child, the Oracle of Delphi foretold that this son was destined to kill his father and take his throne! So Laius decided to take drastic measures. He pierced the flesh of his infant son's feet and bound them together with a long metal pin. He then gave the child to a shepherd, to leave him on a mountain to die. The shepherd, feeling sorry for the baby, put the infant into the care of a Corinthian shepherd who in his turn delivered him to the royal couple of the kingdom of Corinth.

King Polybus and Queen Merope of Corinth, having no children of their own, adopted the baby. They named him Oedipus (Ancient Greek: Οἰδίπους meaning "swollen foot") and raised him as their own. He is the protagonist of our drama.

Years passed and Oedipus became an adult. One day a drunkard called him a bastard. This hurt him deeply, as he had never suspected he might have been adopted. Looking for answers he went to the Delphi Oracle. There he was to learn of the shocking destiny that lay before him. He was told he would kill his father, marry his mother and destroy his native city.

Believing Polybus was his father, Merope his mother and Corinth his city he decided to never set foot there again, in an attempt to avoid this terrible fate. So Oedipus set off to go to another city near Delphi, a city that – without him knowing it – was his real birthplace, Thebes. En route, at a crossroads he had a fight with a man on a chariot. Arguing about who had the right to pass first, the charioteer attempted to run him over. Oedipus killed him and his entourage, sparing the life of just one.

Little did he know that by doing so, he was fulfilling the first part of the prophecy. The man he killed was none other than his birth father, Laius, the king of Thebes! Oedipus was now not only a killer, but unwittingly he had committed a patricide (killing his own father) and a regicide (killing a king).

What dawns upon Oedipus is that the reward for his solving the riddle of the Sphinx was tainted with poison. It would also fulfil the second part of the prophecy. The widow queen he took for a wife was his birth mother. The children he had with her were also his brothers and sisters.

The finale sheds a harsh light upon the crime. All is revealed for the spectator – with a particularly tragic twist. The man attempting to solve the crime *is* the criminal. The king assuming the role of the detective, symbolizing at the same time both truth and justice *is* Laius' murderer.[1] And what's worse he is Laius' son.

The revelation hits hard. On discovering she was married to and had children with her firstborn son, Jocasta commits suicide.

Oedipus, using a pin from a brooch on his mother and wife's gown, blinds himself and goes into in exile. His children and siblings will not be spared. The two sons will kill each other and both daughters will face horrible deaths.

The first detective story comes to a horrible end for all involved. So, in studying Ingres' painting and knowing the outcome of Oedipus' answer, one can't help but wonder: wouldn't it have been better if the crime had remained unresolved? Wouldn't it have been better for all concerned if the Sphinx had indeed devoured Oedipus before our eyes?

1. Annie Combes, *Agatha Christie, L'écriture du crime*, Paris: Les Impressions Nouvelles, 1989, p. 22.

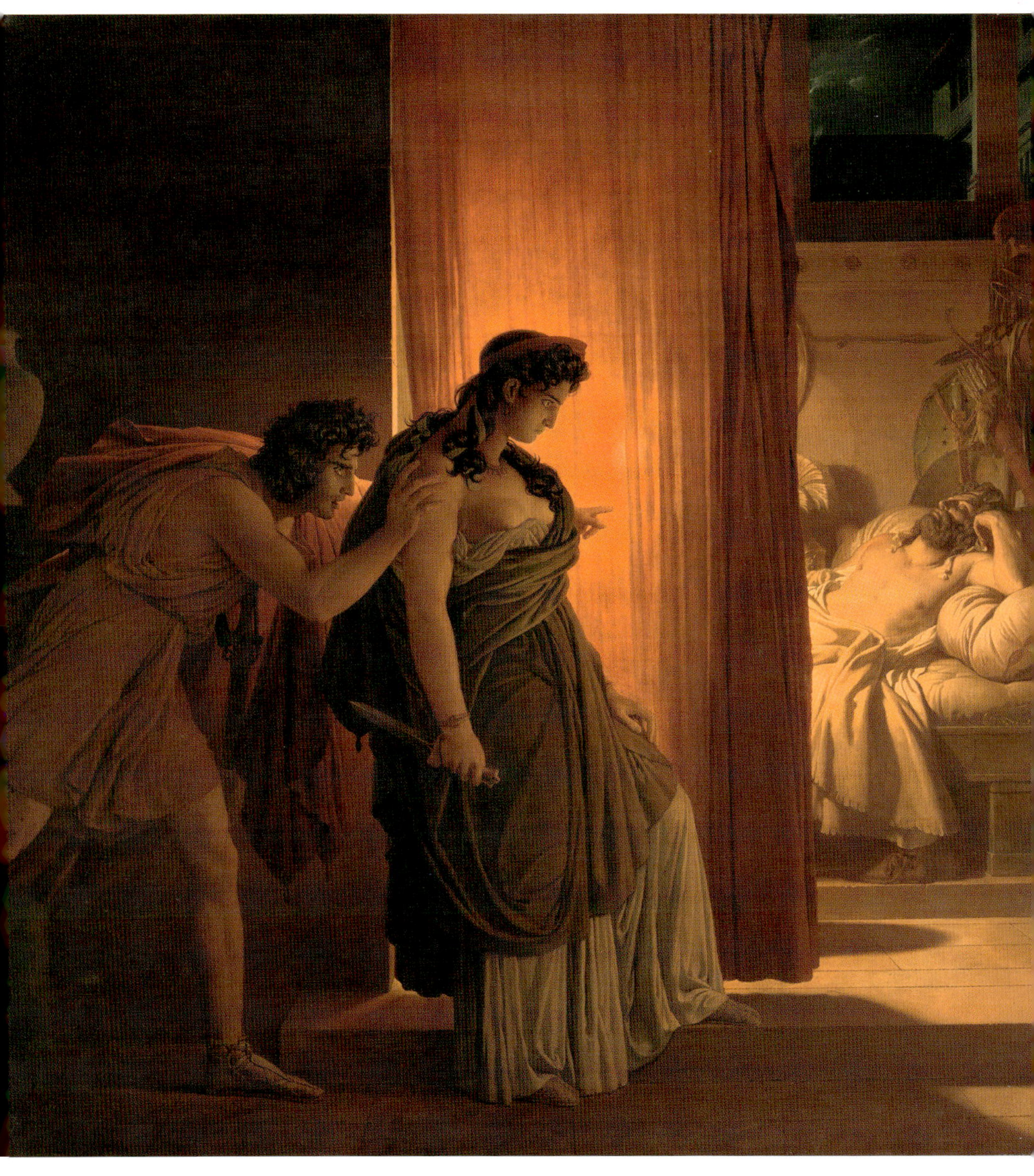

CHAPTER 20
THINKING TWICE

MARITICIDE - WOMEN WHO KILL

Baron Pierre-Narcisse Guérin,
Clytemnestra Hesitates before Killing the Sleeping Agamemnon, 1817
H: 342 cm; L: 325 cm

First Floor, Denon, Daru, Room 75

Family dramas and cursed dynasties are a recurrent theme in ancient Greek myths. The painting before us is a classic example of such a dramatic family affair that would, in time, reduce a whole house to ashes.

Yet, the scene we are witnessing is more complicated than a superficial reading would suggest. It is not the product of a love triangle turned sour. It is not just a crime about power. It's about revenge, betrayal, power, love, greed and defiance.

Under the dim candlelight we see a woman holding a dagger, looking pensively towards a man lying on his bed. Behind her, another man is whispering, pointing and pushing her ever so gently towards the sleeping man. The violent orange light adds to the tension.[1]

The woman in the centre is Clytemnestra, queen of Mycenae[2] and the semi-naked sleeping man she is about to kill is her husband, Agamemnon. Behind her, pushing her to act is her lover Aegisthus, who has been occupying Agamemnon's bed and throne for ten years, while the king was away, fighting the Trojan War. We can see Agamemnon's armour, shield and

---

1. "Guérin. Une belle mise en scène", *Grande Galerie, le Journal du Louvre*, no. 15, March–April–May 2011, p. 90.

2. One of the major centres of Greek civilization in the second millennium BC, situated in the north-eastern Peloponnese.

weapons hung behind him. He was the general of the Greek army, which was victorious against the Trojans and his weapons of war had served him well. But they will not protect him from what is about to happen.

Clytemnestra is pondering between two choices. Her body is leaning backwards, almost reluctant to move towards her sleeping victim. The blade is facing upwards. It is the moment of doubt; it is the moment of hesitation.[1] Will she kill her husband or not? She knows that if she murders him, her fate is determined. Her lover stands behind Clytemnestra reminding her of all that Agamemnon had put her through. He pushes her to be done with it, like the mind pushes the hand to act.[2]

Research tells us that when women commit murder, they are most likely to kill the people closest to them such as intimate partners or other family members. Mariticide is the act of killing one's spouse, with abusive husbands often the victims of household murders committed by women. Was Agamemnon a cruel spouse?

Imagine Clytemnestra in a contemporary courthouse, on the accused's hot seat. Dressed in her royal outfit, her regard is dark and decisive, her voice deep and calm while defending herself to the jury. Her comportment is composed, her arguments well structured.

"I am not afraid of punishment and death, which I know will come, as a result of revenge. I know revenge; I know it all too well. My hand is armed by the same feeling of justice

1. Pierre Sérié, *La Peinture d'histoire en France 1860-1900: La Lyre ou le poignard*, Paris: Arthena, 2014, p. 69.

2. Théophile Gautier, *Guide de l'amateur au Musée du Louvre* (1867), Paris: Nabu Press, 2013.

that will arm my son, Orestes, against me. My fate is sealed, as was his!" she would likely say pointing at her dead husband's body.

"And as is everyone's. Yet I wont be able to tell my son the truth. So when you see him, when he stands before your jury with my blood on his hands, tell him what he ought to know. If he talks of me as an unfaithful wife, a bad mother, hungry for power over which she killed his father, the hero that conquered Troy, tell him this: Agamemnon was no better than me. What he accuses me of, his father had done, yet far worse. It was Agamemnon who murdered my first husband Tantalus and, grabbing the son I had with him from my breasts, threw him against the rocks and killed him. He made me his wife by force, put a crown on my head and his seeds in my fertile soil. He deprived me of a son but gave me three children I loved. So, I started growing fond of him, after all he was my children's father.

But he was a coward, a liar, a general of deception. He told me our daughter Iphigenia was to marry Achilles and for a short time I was the happiest of mothers. But when I arrived for the wedding, they told me my daughter was dead. She was sacrificed by her father. Stabbed in the heart by his own hand so that the Greek army could sail against Troy, looking for Helen, my sister.[1] He sailed to glory and I remained alone in these palaces, mourning for my dead daughter. Hatred started eating me alive. How could I not hate this man who had already killed two of my children? This man who lied, who left

1. Iphigenia was actually saved by the goddess Artemis (Diana in Latin) who replaced her with a deer on the sacrificial altar. Clytemnestra was not aware of this and thought her daughter was dead.

in silence? I was dead, lying in a pit of loathing, until real love made me feel alive again!"

She starts referring to Aegisthus, the man we see in the painting, pushing her towards her destiny. Though female criminals are often victims of persuasion by their male companions, this is not the case here. Clytemnestra is not a pawn. Her voice changes pronouncing her lover's name, it becomes softer. There is even a smile, drawn on her harsh face by pleasant memories.

"Aegisthus loved me and I loved him. We ruled this city for ten years, as was our right, because he had rights to the throne too (see chapter "The Son's Return"). And what's more, he is still on my side, despite the fact that he, too, will die by son's hand. Yet he is here with me, united in life and death.

When Agamemnon came back from Troy, victorious and glorious, what did he expect in his arrogance? That I take him back as husband and King? The killer of my daughter? Should I also ignore that he brought another woman with him, the Trojan princess who bore his two bastard sons? Cassandra was her name and prophesies her game. Yet the oh-so-wise general ignored her begging not to return to Mycenae. She had foreseen they would all die. And they did, for I killed her and her children too.

So, when you see my son, Orestes, when brought before you by the furies[1] for having slain his mother, tell him this: that he avenged the murder of a man who was a killer, an infanticide, a rapist and an adulterer."

---

1. In Greek mythology the Furies or the Erinyes were female spirits of justice and vengeance, pursuing criminals, especially murderers, and driving them mad.

When her plea is over, a modern day jury would possibly be divided. And yet in the "reality" of the myth the decision of a jury would be irrelevant, as her punishment will be death by her own son's hand.

However, there are always two sides to any story. And you have the chance to hear the other side, with Orestes standing before you, on the surface of an ancient Greek vase (See chapter "The Son's Return").

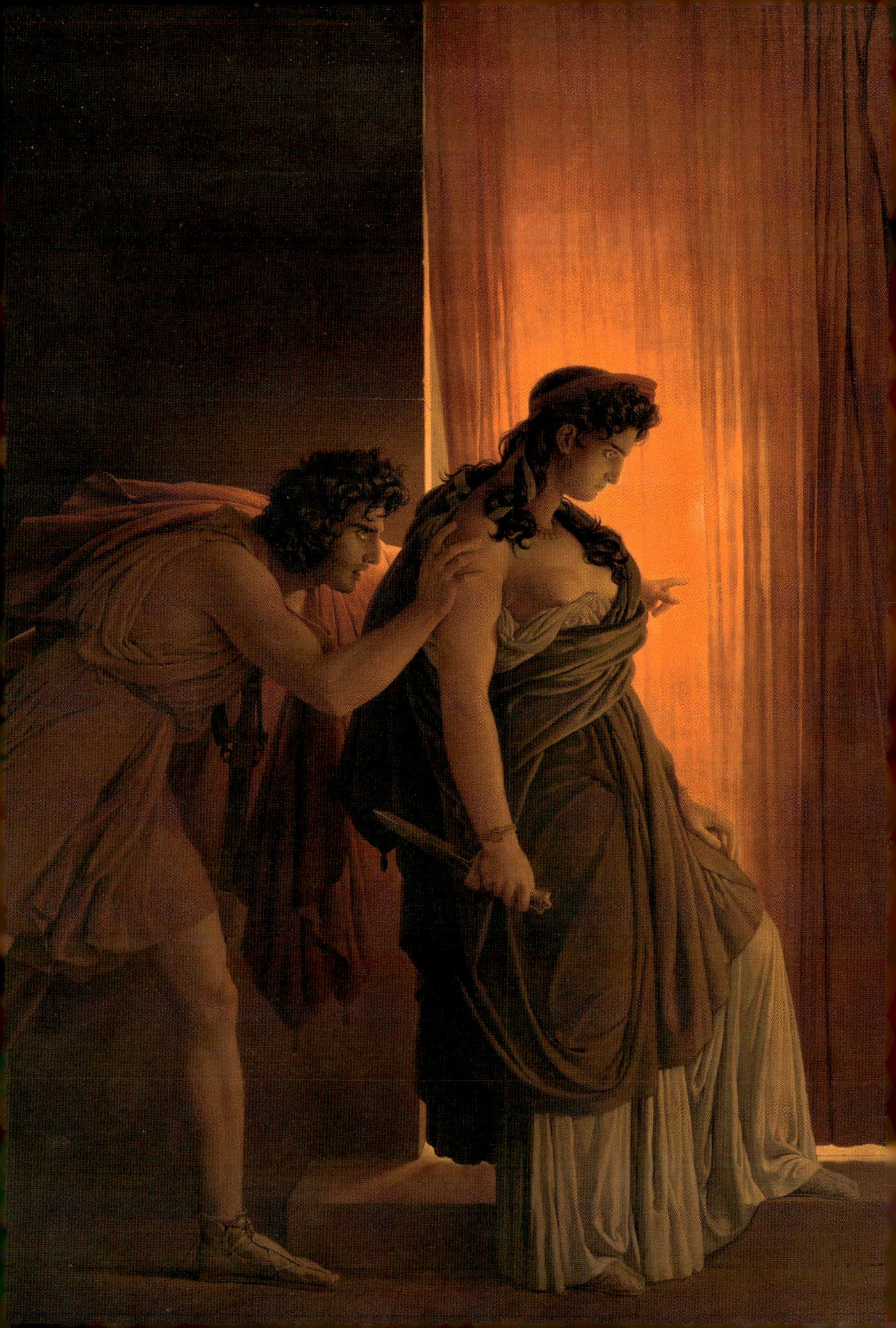

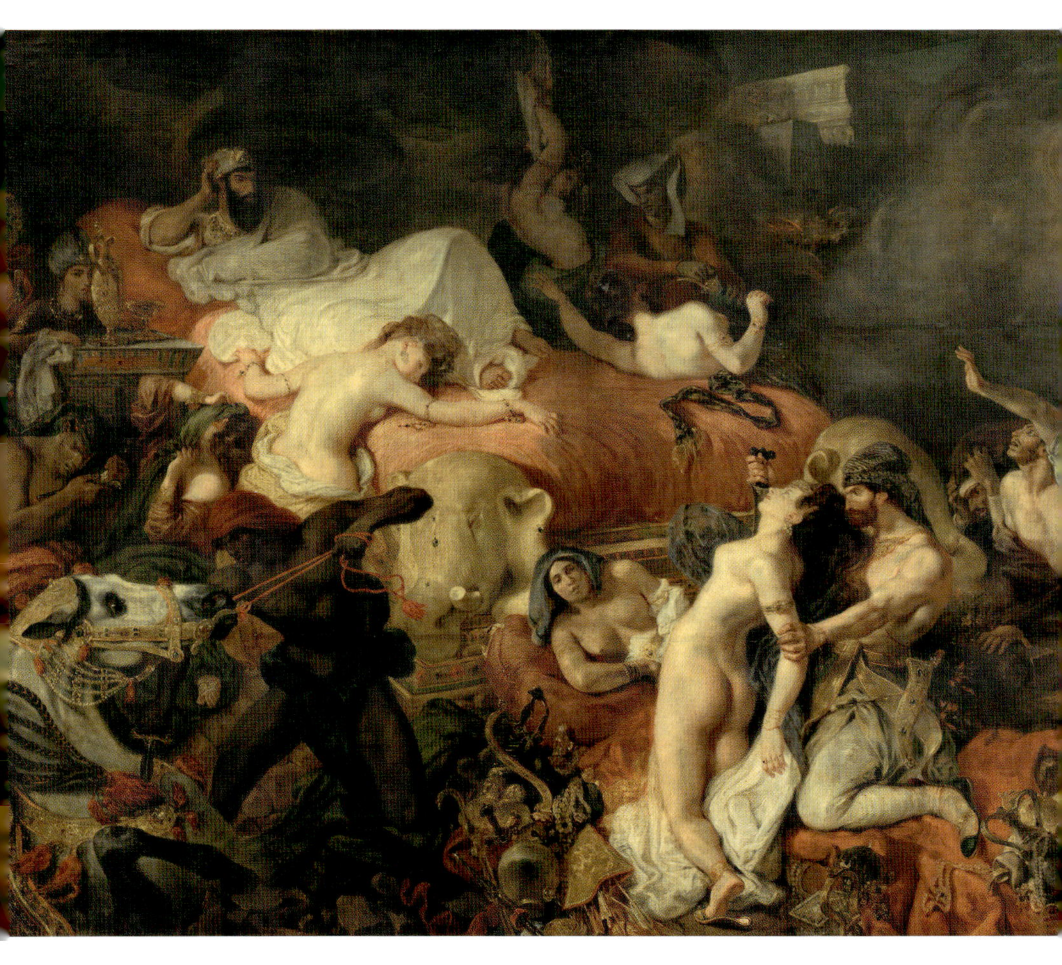

CHAPTER 21
BETTER DEAD THAN SURRENDERED

DEMOCIDE · CRIMINAL LABELLING THEORY

Eugène Delacroix, *The Death of Sardanapalus*, Salon de 1827–28
H: 392 cm, L: 496 cm

First Floor, Denon, Molien, Room 77

Democide is the intentional government killing of an unarmed person or people. It is restricted to intentional killing by a purposive act, policy, process or institution of government, and does not extend to attempts to eliminate cultures, races or a people by means other than killing people as with genocide.[1] According to the theoretician of the concept, R.J. Rummel, "If power kills, absolute power kills absolutely".

Before us on this large canvas we have a chaotic crime scene illustrating such a practice: a despotic leader known as Sardanapalus killing his own people. His name today is synonymous with debauchery and immorality. Yet, as in many crimes, things are not always what they seem to be at first glance.

Delacroix's painting was first presented at the Parisian Salon early in 1828. It created quite a scandal and an outrage with its anarchic synthesis and its graphic violence. Critics considered it "the worst painting of the Salon",[2] a "painter's mistake", pointing to its disorder and chaos, its confusion of lines and colours, its rejection of basic painting principles.[3]

Its theme was inspired by the tragedy "Sardanapalus",

1. R.J. Rummel, *Death by Government*, New Brunswick, New jersey: Transaction Publishers, 1994.
2. *La Gazette de France*, 22 March 1828.
3. Étienne-Jean Delécluze,*Le Journal des débats*, 21 March 1828.

written by Lord Byron in 1821.[1] Yet the scene before us goes beyond the limits of Byron's narrative.

His inspiration for the murderous orgy scene comes from the ancient Sicilian writer Diodorus and his "Historical Library".[2] Diodorus' writings in turn, are based on the work of an ancient Greek physician and historian, Ctesias the Cnidian, and more particularly on his 4th-century BC book series "Persica", where he recounts the history of Assyria, Babylon and the Persian Empire.

According to Ctesias and Diodorus, Sardanapalus lived in the 7th century BC and was the last Assyrian king. Not only was he the last of a line of thirty rulers, he also surpassed all his predecessors in luxury and sloth. In a vast palace in the Empire's capital, a city called Nineveh he lived the life of a woman. His days were spent amongst his concubines weaving wool, masking himself with cosmetics and other ointments used by prostitutes, rendering his skin more delicate than that of any woman. He even spoke as a woman and pursued the greatest pleasures and delights of sexual intercourse with men as well as women, showing not the least concern for the disgrace of such conduct.

He was said to have even written his own epitaph, praising this way of life: "Knowing full well that thou wert mortal born, thy heart lift up, take thy delight in feasts; When dead, no pleasure more is thine. Thus I, who once over mighty Ninus ruled, am naught but dust. Yet these are mine, which gave me

1. Claire Maingon, *Le Salon et ses artistes. Histoire des expositions du Roi Soleil aux Arts Français*, Paris: Hermann Editions, 2009.

2. Diodorus Siculus, *Historical Library. History of India, Scythia, Arabia and the Ocean Islands*, Book II, Paragraphs 23–28.

joy in life – the food I ate, my wantonness, and love's delights. But all those other things men deem felicities, are left behind".

It was precisely this corrupted character and his debauched lifestyle that caused his demise, the destruction of his people and the downfall of the 1,300-year-old Assyrian Empire.

The Medians and the Babylonians under his rule rebelled against him. The uprising was led by two generals, a Median called Arbaces and a Babylonian called Belesys. Their objective was to conquer Nineveh and remove the depraved king.

Despite their numerous military defeats, the rebels persisted. And while Sardanapalus celebrated his victories in his signature hedonistic manner, the generals procured the support of the Arab and the Bactrian peoples. This alliance bore fruit. They started gaining ground and soon had the city of Nineveh surrounded. The king was now trapped within its walls.

Yet he was not worried. The fortification was strong, and supplies were plenty. And in any case, there was an old prophecy saying, "Nineveh would only fall if Tigris – the river around it – would turn against its people". And this could never happen. Or so he thought. Three years into the siege, the river overflowed from heavy rainfall, and the city walls were destroyed, leaving Nineveh prey to the rebels.

Sardanapalus then realized it was all over. But he would not surrender. He would not let himself, nor his precious possessions and the people who served his pleasures fall into his enemies' hands. So "he built an enormous pyre in his palace, heaped upon it all his gold and silver as well as every article of the royal wardrobe, and then, shutting his concubines and eunuchs in the room which had been built in the middle of the pyre, he consigned both them and himself and his palace to the flames".[1]

It is this exact moment that Delacroix depicts. As the painter himself describes it, "Lying on a superb bed, atop a vast pyre Sardanapalus instructs his slaves to kill his wives, his servants, even his horses and his favourite dogs: no objects that had served his own pleasures should outlive him". Observing the painting, there is no escape, no rest for our eyes, just as for the people depicted. Wherever we look in this theatrical scene, we see violence, death, madness, fear and despair.

At the lower right corner a servant stabs a naked woman. As the dagger enters her chest, her last breath leaves her voluptuous body. The last remnants of her life of luxury are her jewels and the sandal posed on the ground, as if anchoring this chaotic scene.[2]

The bedroom is flooded with objects: golden carafes, Oriental jewels, vases, fruits, velvet and silk garments. A place of sexual orgies, as described by the ancient authors, has become a place of carnage.[3]

Yet sensuality is omnipresent. All the victims are naked or semi-naked. Sardanapalus' favourite servant Myrrha is seen collapsed on his bed, her arms in an open cross, already dead. On the opposite side of the bed, a woman hangs herself from a curtain, as if to prevent a death by sword, a fate about to befall the concubine next to her.

---

1. Ibid., Paragraph 27.
2. Gérard Boittelle, *La Mort de Sardanapale: pour une sandale au pied d'une esclave.* https://gboittelle.files.wordpress.com/2010/10/sardanapale-1.pdf
3. "Inventing Assyria: Exoticism and Reception in 19th-Century England and France", Frederick n. Bohrer, *The Art Bulletin*, LXXX, no. 2, June, 1988, pp. 342–56.

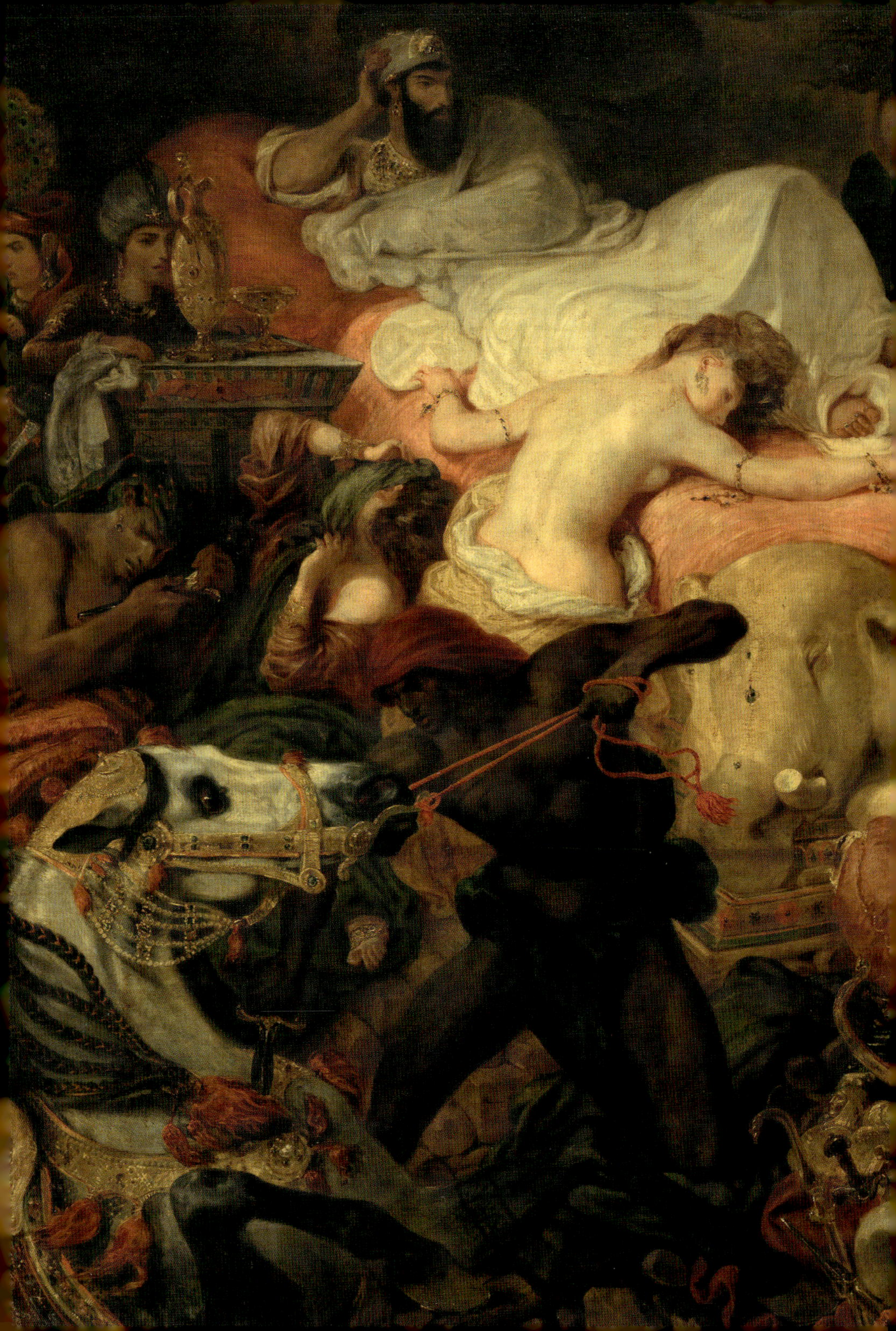

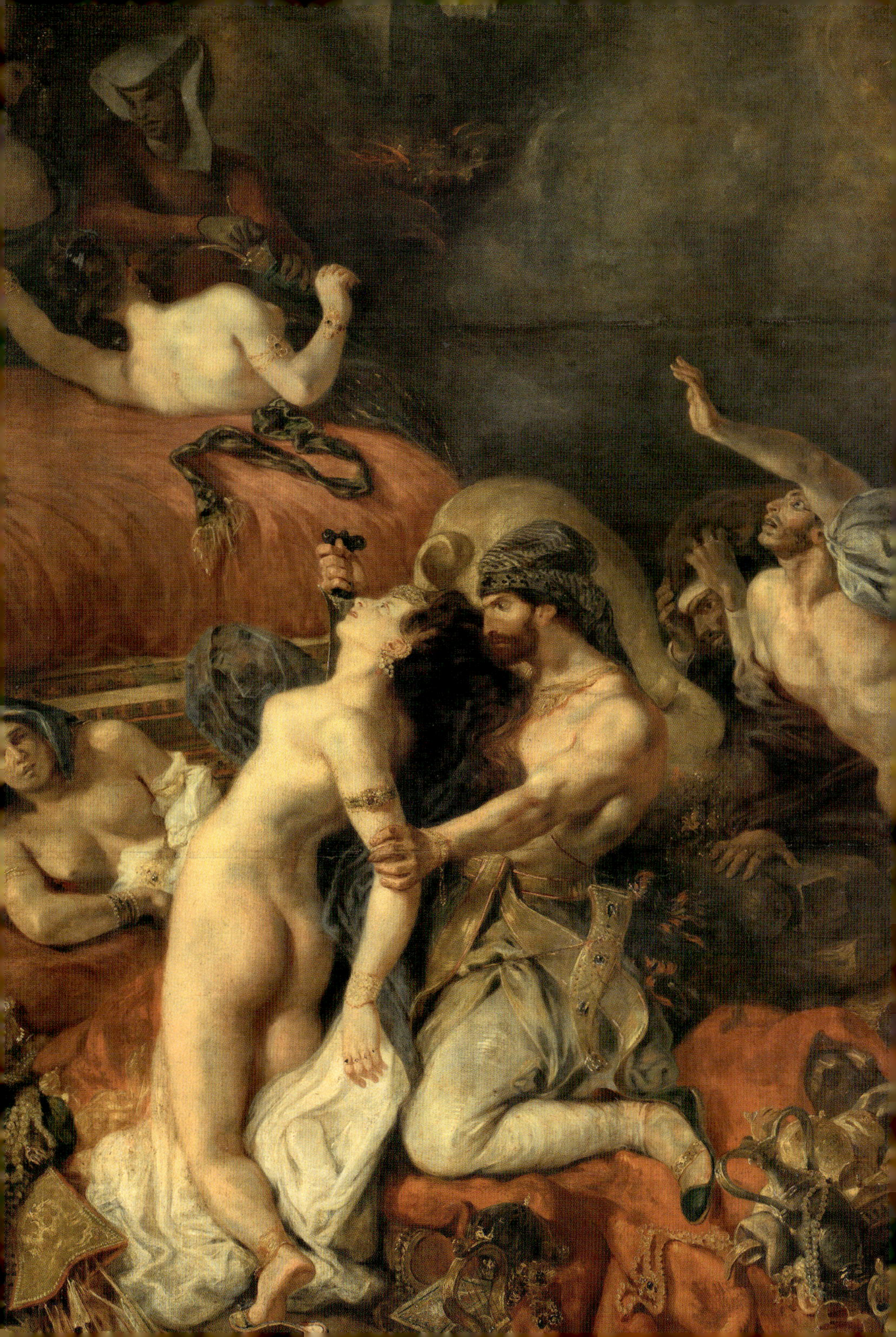

On the left of Myrrha, a woman covers her face to shield her impending death at the hands of an approaching servant. Under her, a slave slays a horse, its eyes full of terror. So are the eyes of the man on the extreme right of the painting. He looks to Sardanapalus, his hand outreached in a pleading gesture.

The whole painting appears to be in movement. It is about to swallow us into its colourful chaos, its spiral of orange, gold, red and flesh – just like the fire and smoke encroaching upon us from the burning city in the background.

We see death, but we can also smell it. We can almost hear the screams. Paradoxically in this bloody orgy, we don't see a single drop of blood. Rather it is symbolized by the red wave of fabric splitting the painting diagonally,[1] beginning at the king's bed and flowing towards us. The source of light follows the reverse path. It leads us from the bottom right to the top left and towards the King's face.[2]

Amongst this dramatic confusion and immeasurable violence, Sardanapalus' serene and indifferent expression underscores the disorder of the scene. He is at the same time judge and executioner; he is the director, the actor and a spectator of this massacre.[3] His inexpressive face is proof of his alleged debauchery, irrationality, self-indulgence and despotism.

Yet history tells a far different story from this depiction and its sources. Sardanapalus as we came to know him, as we see him before us, his story and his fall do not conform to historical facts. Even his name is the Greek phonetic interpretation

1. As in footnote 2 page 147.

2. Barthélemy Jobert, "Étude de tableau, Delacroix, *La mort de Sardanapale*", *Beaux-Arts*, Dec. 1995.

3. www.louvre.fr

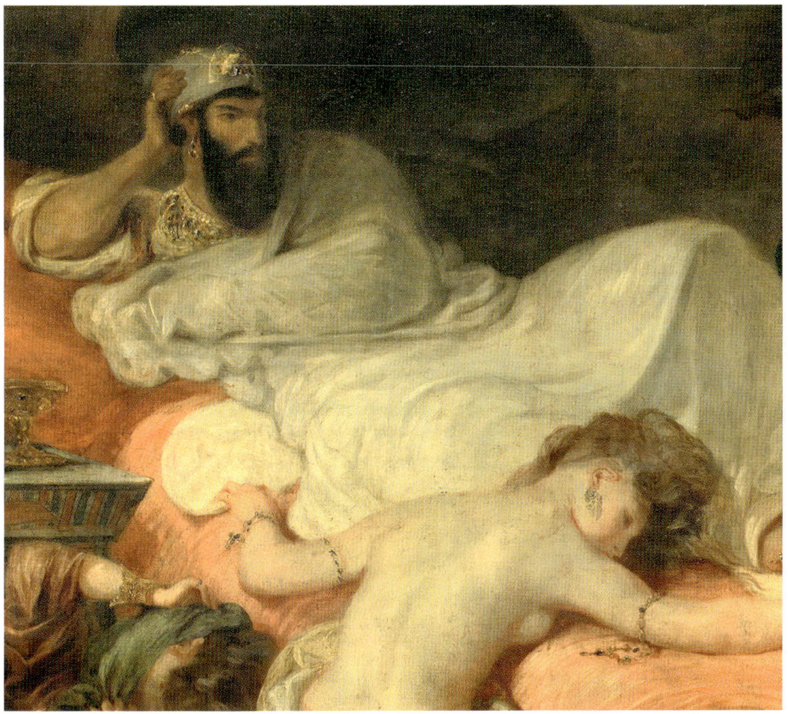

of the name Ashurbanipal, the last *great* king of the Assyrian Empire.

Furthermore, Ashurbanipal bares no resemblance to the labels the Greek historian Ctesias had attributed to Sardanapalus, which were later adopted by Diodorus. In truth Ashurbanipal was a great military leader and an educated ruler, who died of natural causes in 627 BC.

So how, and why, did Ashurbanipal morph into this Sardanapalus character? It seems Ctesias was not very thorough with checking his sources. When writing his account of history, he mixed the characteristics of many Assyrian kings and events from different periods. He did so with a moral filter – critical of the Oriental lifestyle, considered barbaric by Greek standards. Furthermore, he added fictitious elements to make his story even more appealing and give it a moral lesson: Excessive luxury and immorality cause demise.

As a result, Ctesias' reliability was questioned even back then. According to a Greek satirist called Lucian of Samosata, "the people who suffered the greatest torment in hell were those who had told lies when they were alive and written mendacious histories; among them Ctesias of Cnidus."[1]

The vices attributed to the king by Ctesias and Diodorus, and his apathetic face depicted in the painting, bring to mind a criminological theory created by Howard Becker in 1963, called the Labeling Theory.[2]

According to this theory, people may become criminals when labelled as such and when they accept this label as a personal identity. In other words, when someone is labelled a deviant, it is difficult to remove this label from them. A person stigmatized as a criminal or deviant is likely to accept the label, seeing himself as deviant and acting in a way that fulfils the expectations of that label.

We look at Sardanapalus' detached expression towards the chaos he created, his cold and peaceful look towards the victims he ordered killed, showing a lack of empathy, attributed to sociopaths and (serial) killers. It seems that Sardanapalus has indeed accepted the labels the two historians had ascribed to him.

---

1. Lucian of Samosata, *A True Story*, 2.31.
2. H. Becker, *Outsiders: Studies in the Sociology of Deviance*, New York: The Free Press, 1963.

He had become the debauched, ruthless ruler depicted in this painting, fulfilling before our eyes the expectations we, the bloodthirsty and scandal-amused spectators, have of him.

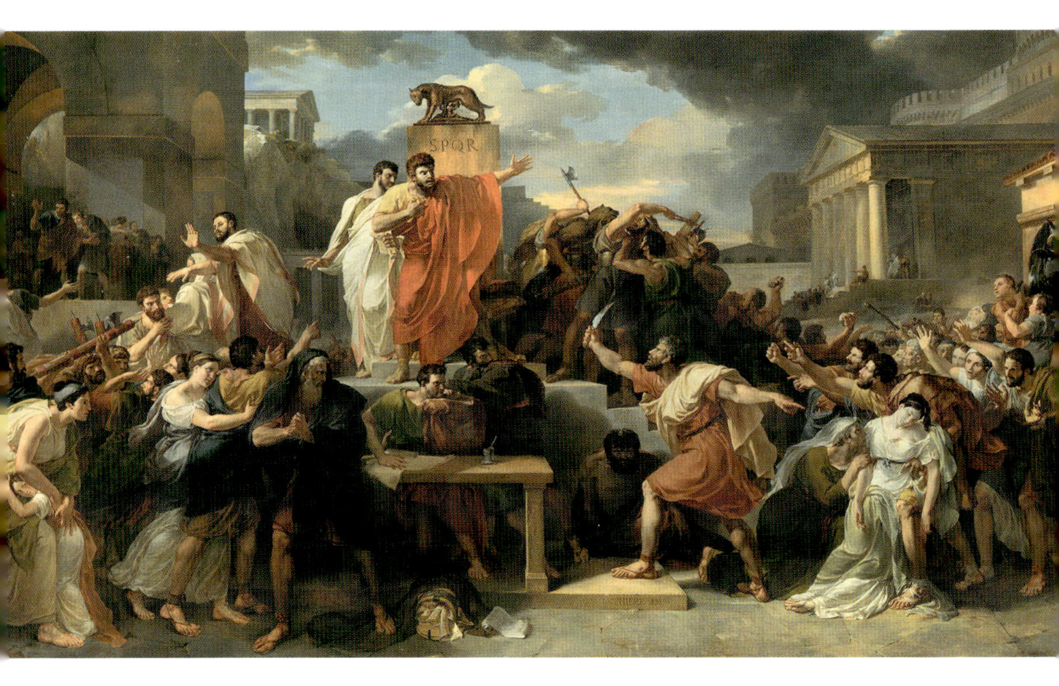
SPQR

CHAPTER 22
THE DAUGHTER'S HONOUR

PREMEDITATED MURDER - CRIME OF PASSION - FILICIDE - HONOUR KILLING

Guillaume Guillon, dit Lethière, *The Death of Virginia*, 1828
H: 458 cm; L: 778 cm

First Floor, Denon, Salon Denon, Room 76

In premeditated murders, the perpetrator has rationally considered all the related factors – when, where and how – before committing the deed, in order to avoid being discovered and arrested. So, it is quite understandable why most of them are committed in secret. Who wants a witness who can identify the murderer?

On the opposite end of premeditation stand crimes of passion, the crimes that are committed in the heat of the moment by someone unable to control their strong impulses, such as sudden rage, jealousy, fear or heartbreak. These crimes are often played out in front of bystanders. That is the scenario before us, to which we stand witness along with the Romans in the painting.

A young woman on the right, dressed in white, leans on the hands of a man and an old maid. Her pale skin, the abandonment of her body and the blood stain on her chest above her heart, combined with the bloody knife held by the man in the orange tunic leave no doubt. This woman is dead, murdered by the man, whose finger is pointing at her, rattling the weapon towards the men on the pedestal.

The statue of a female wolf feeding Romulus behind the latter along with their surroundings indicate we are in the forum of ancient Rome. The crowd that has witnessed the murder is shocked, horrified and anxious. We can sense their anger in their movement.

Yet neither their posture, their aggressive – almost theatrical – gestures[1] as their hands form fists or pick up stones and arms, nor their furious looks are directed towards the killer. Rather, they create a violent pyramid towards the two men on the platform.

One of these two men is dressed in a red toga, making his face appear even paler. His name is Appius Claudius Crassus, a patrician[2] who, serving as a decimvir, [3] had provided written laws to the people. The very same laws he later blatantly disregarded. Looking over his shoulder is one of his clients,[4] Marcus Claudius who served as his pawn in the scheme that resulted in the girl's death.

The victim's name is Virginia, daughter of Lucius Virginius, a roman centurion.[5] He is the one holding the knife, and the killer of his own daughter. He committed a filicide, in order to spare his daughter from dishonour. According to Human Rights Watch, "Honour killings are acts of vengeance, usually death, committed by male family members against female family members, who are held to have brought dishonour upon the family." This case though is slightly different: the killing is committed to prevent the dishonouring of the virgin daughter.

The year is 449 BC. Virginia is sixteen years old and, on

1. "Ouverture du Salon", *Le Courrier Français*, 2 May 1831, B.N. Micr. D124, 1° Article.
2. A person of noble or high rank.
3. Member of a board or a commission of ten members.
4. Clients were peasant farmers who rented land and followed a certain patron, performing duties for him.
5. The commander of a *centuria*, the smallest unit of a Roman legion.

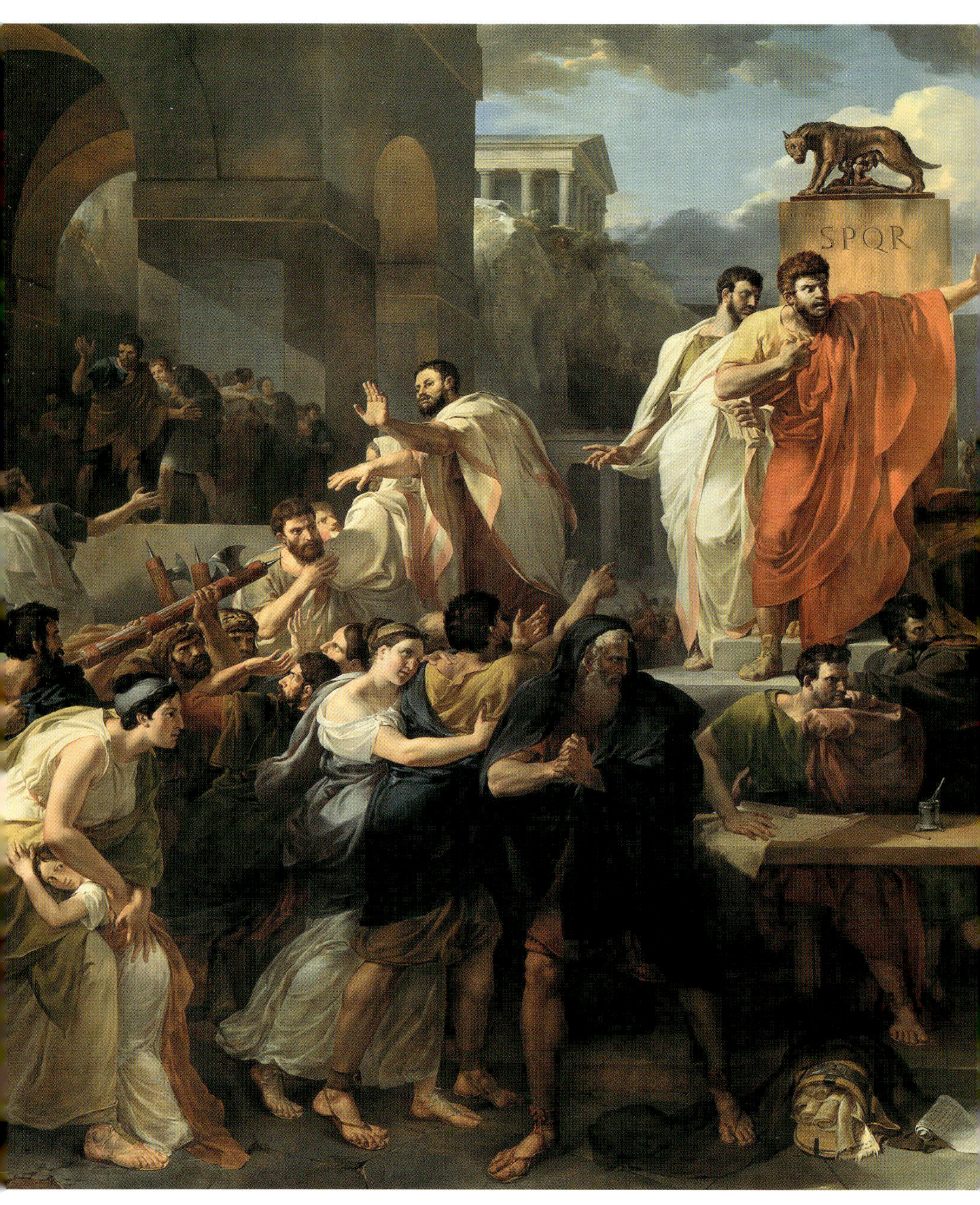
SPQR

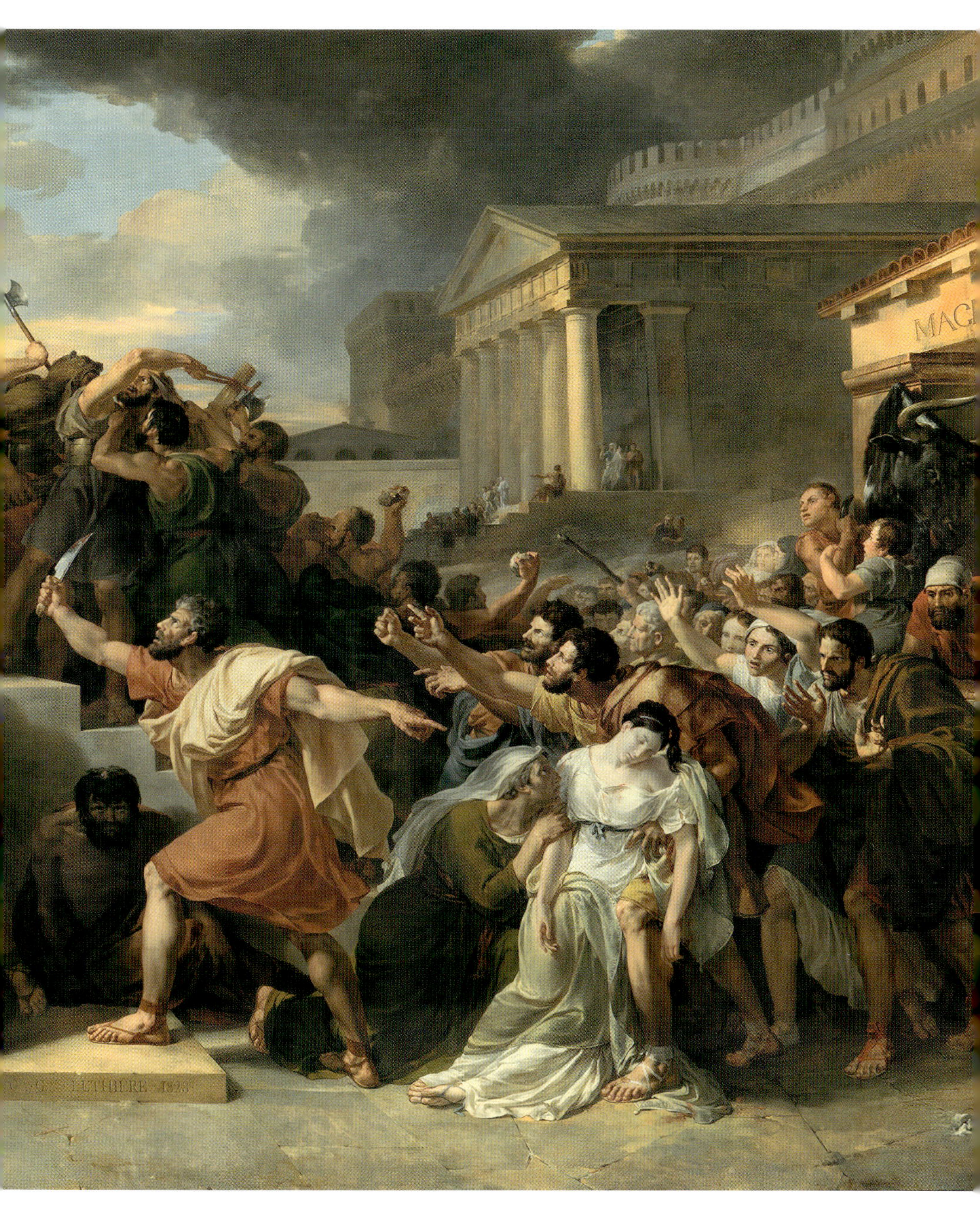
MAC
LETHIERE 1828

her way to school, Appius Claudius Crassus sees her and falls in love with her. To make her his own, he weaves a devious plan. He demands Marcus Claudius (standing behind him) to proclaim that Virginia was not her parents' biological child, but rather the daughter of a slave of his, later adopted by Lucius Virginius and his wife. Since the mother slave belonged to Marcus Claudius, her child too is his property.

Appius Claudius was to be the judge in this case, deciding whether Virginia belonged to Marcus Claudius or not. Appius Claudius chose his timing well. The case was to be decided during her father's absence away in the battlefield. He pretended to call for Lucius Virginius in order to defend his case, and in the meantime, breaking his own laws, he would award his client Marcus Claudius temporary possession of Virginia.

Despite the obstacles imposed by Appius Claudius who had sent a message to the camp to stop him from returning, Lucius Virginius managed to reach Rome in time. Violating his own laws and without any sense of justice, Appius Claudius awarded the sixteen-year-old maiden to his client.[1] The same night she would be in his own bed.

Her father would not stand for it. He asked permission to speak to her one last time. He then took a knife he found on a butcher's bench and killed her.[2] It was the only way to defend her and the family's honour.

Amongst the angry mob, on the far left of the painting a mother is holding her daughter tightly in her arms. She is not

1. Titus Livius (Livy). *History of Rome*. (Ab Urbe Condita) English Translation by. Rev. Canon Roberts. New York, New York: E. P. Dutton and Co., 1912, Book 3.44.

2. Arlette Sérullaz, "Douze Dessins de Lethière au Louvre", *Études, La revue des Musées de France, Revue du Louvre*, 1-2005, p. 78.

protecting her from the murderer, but from the city officer. No girl is safe anymore; no law is sufficient to protect justice and moral values.

But the crowd supporting Lucius Virginius, has risen. The Patricians, standing on higher ground in their white togas try to calm the mob while their guards try to protect them. They will not succeed. Virginius will be arrested but his followers will soon free him, Appius Claudius and the decemvirate will be overthrown and the Roman Republic re-established.

This is not the last time in our Louvre Tour that we will see a parent killing their offspring. It is a repeating motif, whether committed for justice, honour or revenge.

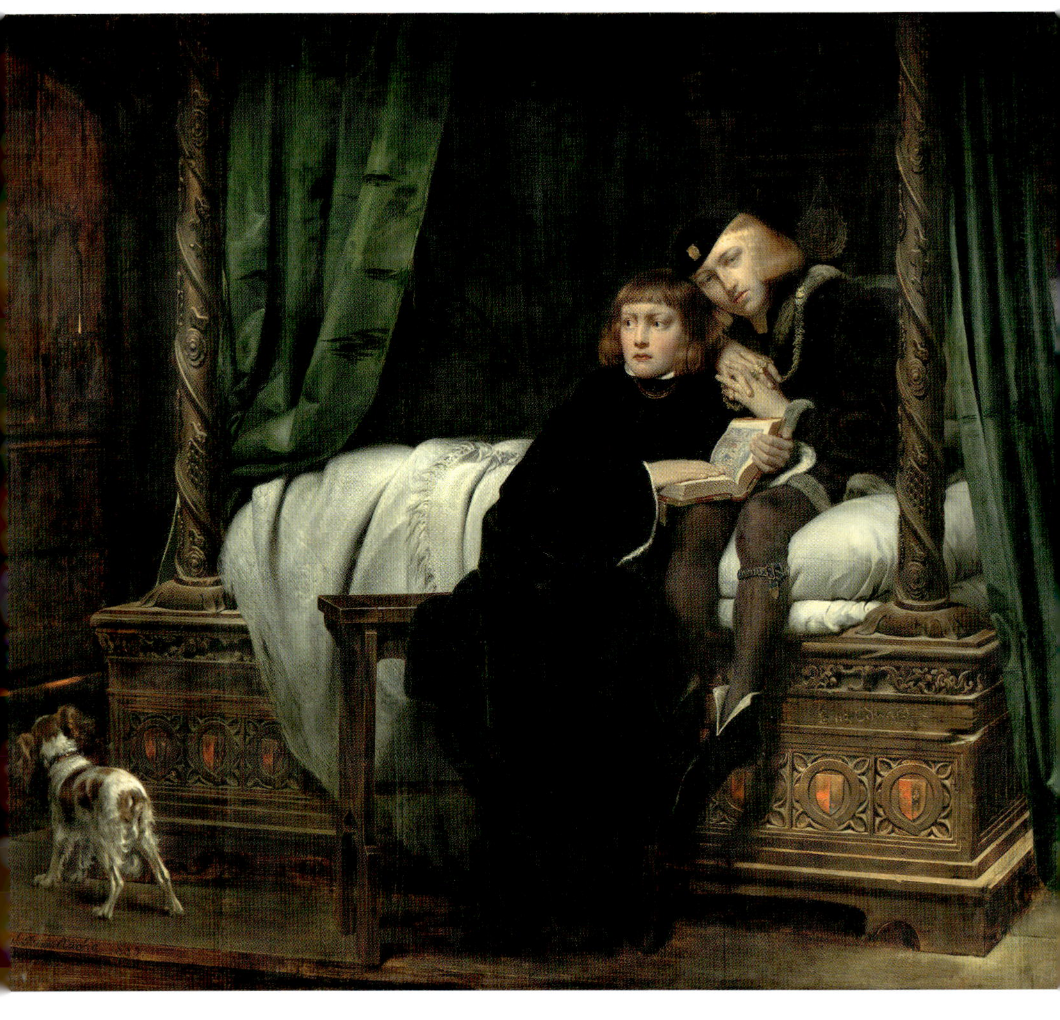

CHAPTER 23
THE KING IS MURDERED, LONG LIVE THE MURDERER

REGICIDE - DNA TESTING

Paul Delaroche, *King Edward V and the Duke of York in the Tower of London*, 1831
H: 181 cm; L: 215 cm

First Floor, Denon, Mollien, Room 77

The craving for power has been a consistent motive for murder over the ages. Whether it be ancient Egypt or Rome, Byzantium or medieval Europe, killing a ruler to usurp their position of power was by no means an unusual phenomenon. The killing of a king (and by extension a queen) is called regicide. Although the would-be king is almost always the initiator, the actual murder is not often committed by his own hand. More commonly the deed is executed by others.

The painting before us is the artist's interpretation of one of England's most controversial questions: the fate of Edward IV's children. And Delaroche's answer, based on Shakespeare's Richard III is the scene we are witnessing.[1]

A regicide is about to be committed. The king about to be murdered, along with his younger brother, is just a child: the thirteen-year-old Edward V. Though he was never officially crowned, his eighty-six-day reign began with his father's death on 9 April 1483. It ended on June 26 when his uncle Richard, the Duke of Gloucester, who had been appointed Lord Protector, was crowned king under the name Richard III.

Before his uncle's illegitimate coronation, the young king

1. Beth Segal Wright "Scott and Shakespeare in 19th Century France", *Arts Magazine* 55, Feb. 1981, p.129.

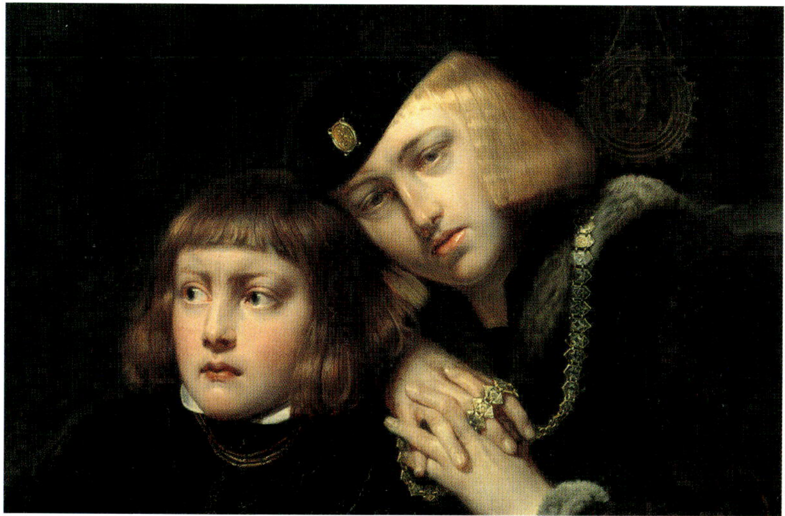

was imprisoned with his nine-year-old brother, Richard of Shrewsbury, the Duke of York, in the Tower of London. Rarely seen from the beginning of his short reign, the boy and his brother completely disappeared in late summer of the same year. Although their fate is officially unknown, it is strongly believed that they were killed under their uncle's orders, in his attempt to secure the throne.

Edward V, who we can recognize by his garter, is seated on the bed in this sumptuously decorated room. He looks at us, the only witnesses to his last moments. His sense of calm and his stoic regard are the hallmarks of a king. By contrast the fear on his brother's face is evident.[1] Leaning towards Edward and holding a book, his eyes are directed towards the door, where the sound of approaching assassins can be heard.

1. Stephen Bann in Exh. cat., *Paul Delaroche, Un Peintre dans l'Histoire* – Nantes, Musée des Beaux-Arts, 22 October 1999 – 17 January 2000, p. 23.

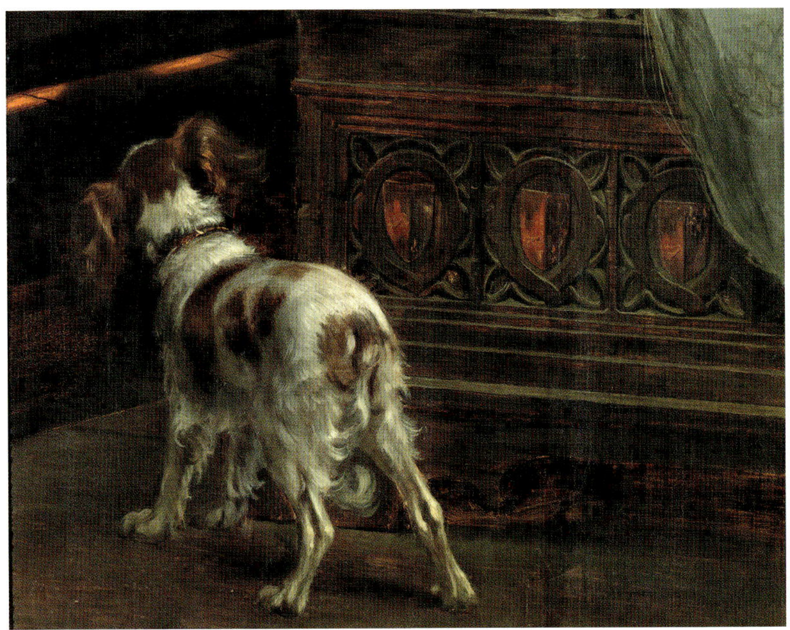

The ambiance of fear and impending doom is underscored by their spaniel, with its ears pricked up and tail between its legs.[1] The light under the door and the shadow of a foot behind it make the threat even more imminent. Whoever is behind this door will go on to smother the two children to death, in the prime of their youth, so that their uncle may secure the throne.[2]

After their murder, no one knows what happened to their bodies. In 1674, workmen remodelling the Tower of London

1. François Nourissier, Élisabeth Foucart-Walter, *Chiens*, Paris: Musée du Louvre Editions –Flammarion, 2007.

2. Jean Galard, *Promenades au Louvre : En compagnie d'écrivains, d'artistes et de critiques d'art*, Paris: Robert Laffont (Bouquins), 2010, p. 713.

found a wooden box buried three metres under a staircase. The box contained two small human skeletons. The bones were examined in 1933. By measuring certain bones and teeth, the examinations concluded that they belonged to two children around the same ages as the murdered princes. Despite the controversy and with the remains of their uncle Richard III recently discovered, to date no DNA testing has been performed on these skeletons to confirm or exclude the possibility that they truly belong to the princes. As DNA is present through the family bloodlines down many generations, DNA testing is used when no other form of identification – through dental records, fingerprints, clothing, blood tests etc. – is available.

The representation of Edward V, the age and innocence of the young king, his unofficial and pointless reign that ended before it essentially began and his dramatic ending, allude to another case of regicide. It involves the death of another legitimate sovereign,[1] a young king closer to Delaroche's time and geography: Louis the XVII.

He was the son of Louis XVI and Marie Antoinette. Born in 1785 he became, according to the dynastic order, king of France after his father's execution in 1793. His title, which meant nothing in the newly born Republic, accompanied him to his death by maltreatment in the Temple prison in 1795. Louis XVII was only ten years old.

1. Marie-Claude Chaudonneret, "Du genre anecdotique au genre historique. Une autre peinture d'histoire", in Exh. cat *Les Années romantiques*, Nantes: Musée des Beaux-Arts, Paris: Galeries Nationales du Grand Palais, Plaisance: Palazzo Gotico 1995–96, p. 83.

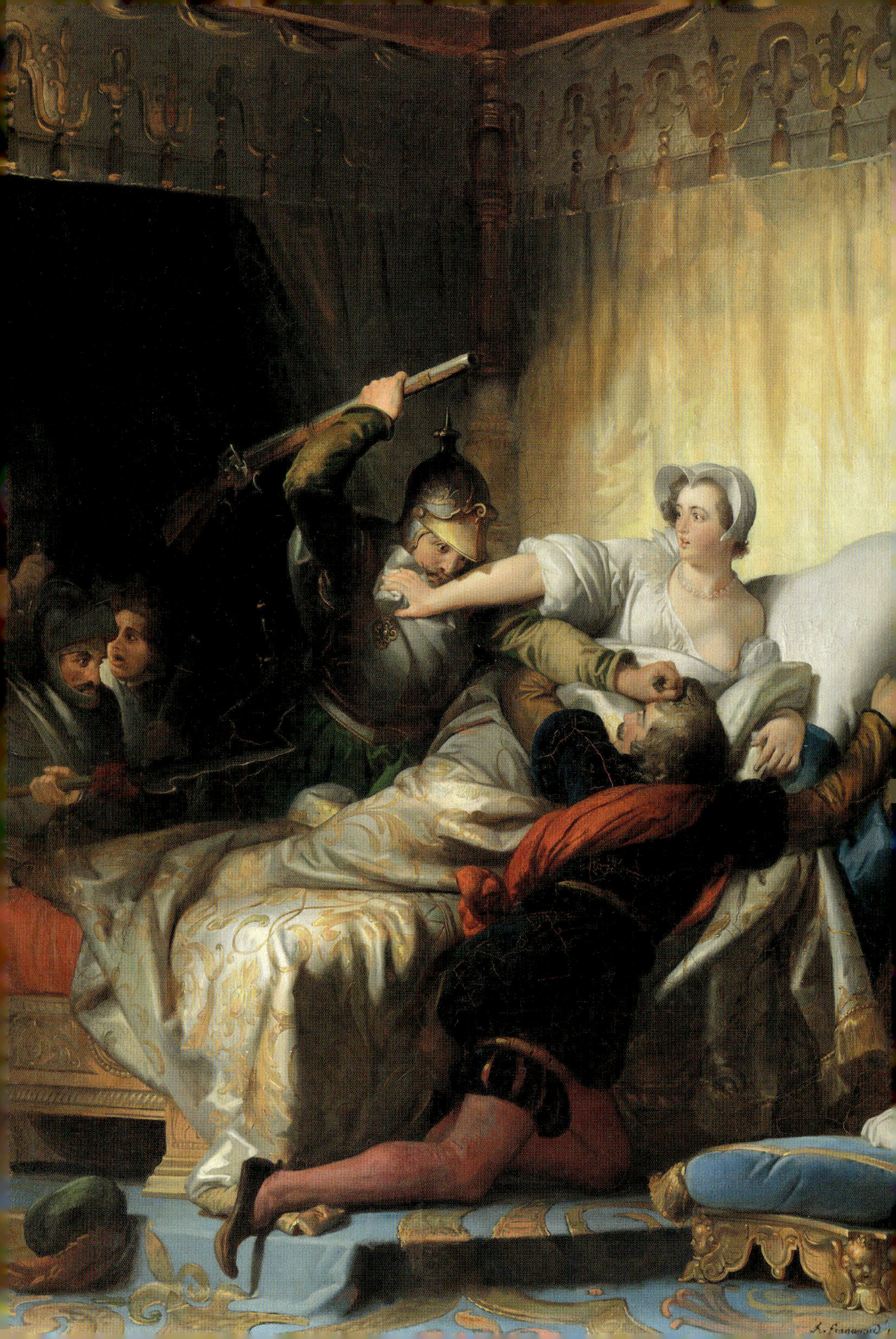

CHAPTER 24

SACRED NIGHT, BLOODY NIGHT

MASSACRE · GENOCIDE

Alexandre-Evariste Fragonard,
Scene of the Saint-Bartholomew Massacre, 1836
H: 179 cm; L: 133 cm

Second Floor, Sully,
Romantic Idylls and Dramas (1820–35), Room 66

The night of the Saint-Bartholomew massacre is the most notorious episode of the War of Religions (1562–98) between French Catholics and Protestants. Beyond the excuse of warfare, we see in this massacre an episode among many that have outlined an attempt at the systematic extermination of a group for religious reasons. By adopting contemporary terminology, the acts that marked the wars of religion – such as killing the members of a group for what they are and not for what they did, causing them serious bodily harm, forcing them to convert into another group – acts committed with intent – for which there is no need for direct State orders as this intent can also be concluded from a systematic pattern of coordinated acts – correspond to the definition of genocide adopted by the General Assembly of the United Nations in 1948.[1] The two paintings before us illustrate two different

1. According to The Convention on the Prevention and Punishment of the Crime of Genocide (CPPCG) which was adopted by the UN General Assembly in 1948, Genocide is: Any of the following acts committed with intent to destroy, in whole or in part, a national, ethnical, racial or religious group, as such: killing members of the group; causing serious bodily or mental harm to members of the group; deliberately inflicting on the group conditions of life, calculated to bring about its physical destruction in whole or in part; imposing measures intended to prevent births within the group; [and] forcibly transferring children of the group to another group.

scenes of the night that became infamous as the peak of the Parisian Huguenots'[1] carnage.

A royal marriage which was to celebrate the reconciliation between the two warring factions, turned instead into a bloodbath that started within the walls of the Louvre, which was then the Royal Palace. The bloodbath began on the night of 23–24 August 1572, on the eve of the feast of the apostle Bartholomew. And from the palace it expanded to the whole of Paris and then throughout France.

In 1572, Catherine de' Medici, the Queen Mother of France arranged to marry her daughter Margaret de Valois, to the Protestant prince, Henry of Navarre, in order to put an end to years of civil conflicts within the kingdom. The wedding, condemned by traditionalist Catholics and the Pope, nevertheless took place on 18 August in Paris, drawing many noble Protestants into a deeply Catholic and anti-Protestant city.

On 22 August a Huguenot nobleman, the Admiral Gaspard de Coligny was shot and seriously wounded, while returning to his home from the Louvre. Though it is still not clear who was behind his attempted assassination, theories include suspects such as the Duc de Guise (a prominent Catholic figure) and Catherine de' Medici herself. Regardless, this act triggered the bloody events to come.

As fear of Protestant retaliation grew, King Charles IX succumbed to the pressure from his advisors and his mother Catherine de' Medici, to kill Huguenot leaders in order to avoid yet another civil war. But Charles went even further. He gave the order to kill every Huguenot, so that no one,

---

1. French Protestants, mainly Calvinist of the 16th and 17th centuries.

according to his paranoid thinking, would reproach him for the deed.

The first painting depicts a scene, taking place in the Palace of the Louvre, in Margot de Valois' opulently decorated bedroom. It's the middle of the night. The young French princess, and through marriage Queen of Navarra, has just been awakened by a violent knocking on the door. The man falling in front of her bed has been searching for Margot's husband. His name is Tejan. He is a Protestant and a servant of Henry of Navarra.[1] He has been running for his life through the long corridors of the Louvre looking for safety. The Catholic soldiers have pursued him and as with every Huguenot within the palace, their intention is to execute him. In the painting we see them having entered the room. One has him in his grip and is about to strike him with the stock of his gun.

Amongst the soldiers, Margot's maid defines the tension of the forced entrance and the violence of the scene by her shocked and bewildered expression. Queen Margot, her mistress, upright in her bed; her cheeks flushed red, her white breast revealed, is moved by the powerful plea of Tejan. With her gesture she prevents the soldier from killing him.

The queen is taking matters into her own hands: she demands to know what this man's crime is. She will judge his fate, whether he is to be handed over to the soldiers or not.

"He is a Protestant. The king ordered to kill them all" is the soldier's response. His answer shocks her. Her thoughts at this moment must have fled to her protestant husband and his

1. *An Awful Warning or The Massacre of Saint Bartholomew, Inscribed to the memory of the late Rt. Hon Spencer Perceval*, London, 1812, p. 25.

fate. Is he still alive? The outcome of this scene is that Margot refuses to hand Tejan over, defying her brother's orders.

"If you wish to kill him, you'll have to kill me first" she is believed to have said. Killing a French Catholic princess, daughter and sister of French kings, was not an option, so the soldiers left her room without their prey. Margot played a crucial part during this night of horror, by protecting other Protestants in her bedroom. Amongst those spared, was her husband Henry, who was to later become Henry IV, King of France.[1]

In the second painting we see another scene from the massacre, taking place some hours later than the scenario illustrated in the first picture, as the light of dawn streaming in from the open window indicates. Among the members of the extermination squad is a soldier, a monk and a man with a white cross on his helmet – a symbol of distinction that ensured he would not be mistaken for a Huguenot. In the painting they have forced themselves into the room of another highly positioned Protestant named Briou. The signs of struggle are obvious: the hourglass and the open book laying on the floor next to the elderly man, on whose forehead a recent wound can be seen. Briou is the tutor of François de Bourbon, Prince de Conti, who also belongs to a Protestant family.

We see the shocked fourteen-year-old prince attempting to save his governor from the man about to strike him with his knife. The young prince has thrown himself on the floor

1. His reign will last from 1589 to 1610. His marriage to Marguerite de Valois – which left no heirs – will be annulled in 1599. In 1600 he will marry Marie de' Medici, and an heir will be born the next year (the future Louis XIII). Henri IV will be assassinated in 1610. There are theories that his new wife might have been behind his assassination.

to shield his tutor with his body.[1] His attempts however are in vain. The spear above his torso will soon pierce the bearded man.

Briou will face his demise with courage and dignity. He looks fearless and his only reaction to the attack is to push his young master away from him, protecting him from the strikes intended for himself. The Prince de Condi will be obliged to convert to Catholicism some weeks later.

No age or sex was exempt from this massacre. Women, children, old men and infants all faced death at the hands of soldiers or their neighbours. Every and any object was used as a weapon of death. When the bodies of dead Huguenots were thrown into the Seine River, it was said that one could cross the river by stepping on the cadavers.

The Massacre of Saint Bartholomew has remained in collective memory as one of the most infamous incidents of a long-lasting religious genocide. It has also inspired many artists to depict factual or imaginary scenes from this bloody night. Not all of these works are displayed in the Louvre Museum, but in many of them the Louvre Royal Palace is featured in the background. After all it is here where it was planned and it all began.

1. *An Awful Warning*, p. 26.

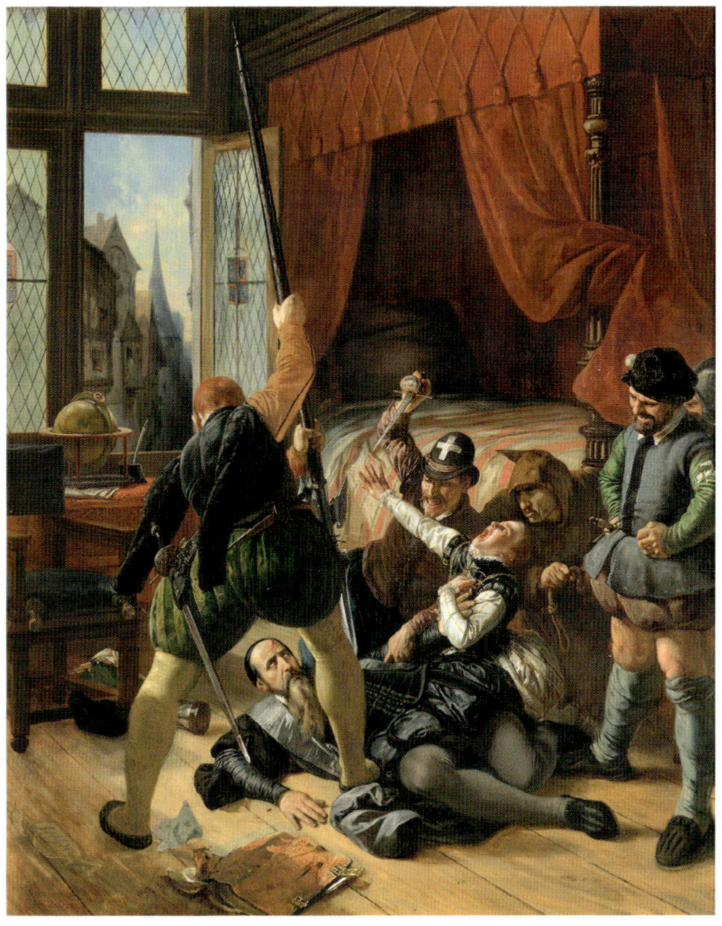

Joseph-Nicolas Robert-Fleury, *Saint Bartholomew's Day Massacre*, 1833
H: 165 cm; L: 130 cm. Second Floor, Sully,
Romantic Idylls and Dramas (1820–35), Room 66

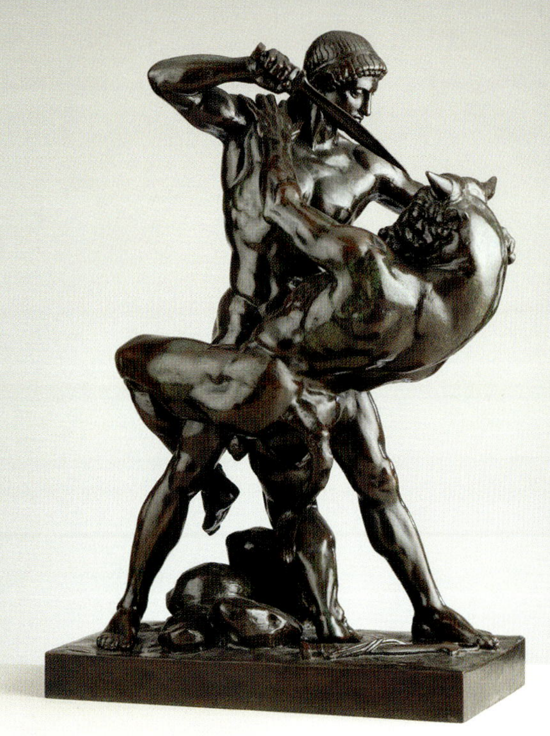

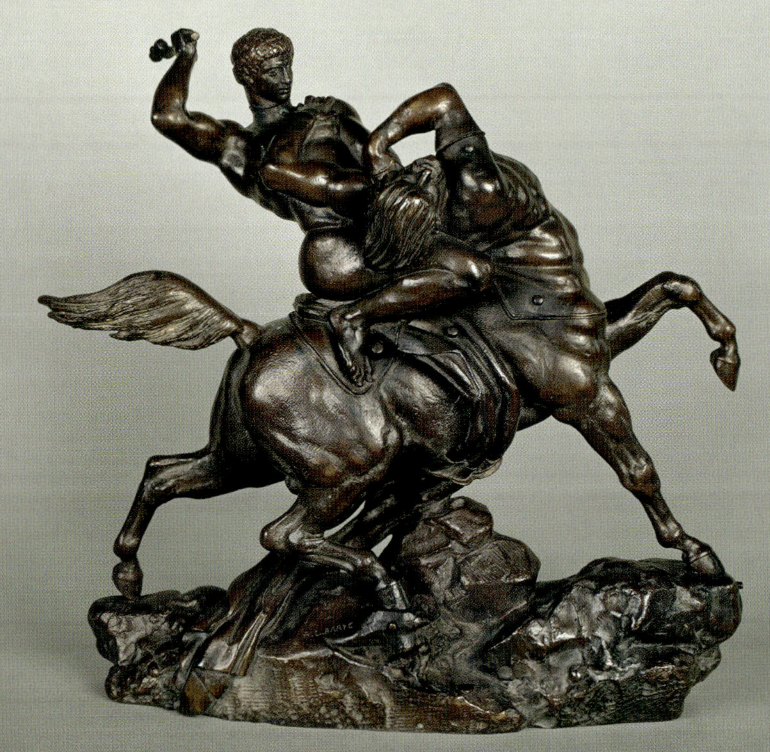

CHAPTER 25
ANTIQUITY'S DEXTER MORGAN[1]

SERIAL KILLER

Antoine-Louis Barye, *Theseus Fighting the Minotaur*,
between 1855 and 1874
Bronze after the plaster model refused at the Salon of 1843,
H: 45 cm; L: 29 cm; D: 17 cm

Antoine-Louis Barye, *Theseus Fighting the Centaur Bianor*, 1877
Bronze, H: 128 cm; L: 113 cm; D: 58 cm

Ground Floor, Richelieu, Barye, Room 33

1. Dexter Morgan is a fictional hero in a books series by Jeff Lindsay and the character of an HBO TV series. He is a forensic analyst working for the police and at the same time a serial killer who targets unpunished murderers.

According to the FBI's Behaviour Analysis Unit, a Serial Killer is an offender who kills two or more victims in separate events.[1] Motives behind a serial killer's act vary from sexual satisfaction to financial gain and power- or attention-seeking. Mostly, they choose a particular type of victim and adopt a specific modus operandi. Their most prevalent and common characteristic is that they are usually sociopaths, lacking empathy, moral responsibility and social conscience.

The killer before us, represented in both sculptures by the same artist, is Theseus, an ancient Greek hero. Seeing him killing two different victims, at two different moments in time, we can't help but wonder: could he be cast as a serial killer?

In the first sculpture we see him fighting with a creature that is half-human, half-bull, the infamous Minotaur. The monster lived in the Labyrinth of the Knossos Palace in Crete, the residence of King Minos. After winning a war over Athens, the Cretan King demanded that the defeated city send seven young maidens and seven young men to be fed to the Minotaur every nine years. Theseus, the son of the Athenian King Aegeus, travelled to Crete and with the help of Ariadne – the daughter of King Minos – he killed the beast.

1. https://www.fbi.gov

The scene before us is the last sequence of this battle. Their bodies are embroiled in a violent struggle.[1] The monster's leg firmly enfolds Theseus' hip, his hand gripping Theseus' shoulder, as he leans back to avoid the hero's sword. On some level they look as if they are dancing a tango, yet this dance will prove deadly for the Minotaur. Soon Theseus' sword will penetrate the bull's scull[2] and Athens will be freed from the blood tax that was imposed upon it by the Cretan King.

The second killing takes place upon a rock. Theseus is riding the back of another mythical creature: half-horse – half-human, known as a Centaur. The hero has the centaur by his neck. The creature desperately attempts to escape his grip, but Theseus has the advantage. Like the Minotaur, the Centaur too will soon lie dead, stricken this time by Theseus' bat. But what has he done to deserve such a violent death?

The Centaurs were invited to the wedding of the Lapith[3] king, Pirithous with Hippodamia. Theseus, Pirithous' friend, was there too. Having tasted wine for the first time, the Centaurs became drunk and aggressive. They attempted to kidnap the Lapithian women, amongst them the bride Hippodamia. The battle that followed was won by the Lapiths, with Theseus fighting on their side. What we see before us is a scene from this fight.

Go back to the initial question: could Theseus be cast as a serial killer? We have the FBI's definition. We have two victims

1. Charles Avery, "From David d'Angers to Rodin – Britain's National Collection of French 19th Century sculpture", *The Connoisseur*, vol. CLXXIX, April 1972, p. 234.

2. Michel Poletti, Alain Richarme, *A.-L. Barye, Artiste et Artisan*, Paris: Univers du Bronze, Sculptures XIXe et XXe, p. 34.

3. The Lapiths were a legendary people of Greek mythology, living in Thessaly, central Greece.

that fit a particular type, i.e. half-men – half-animals. And we have established a pattern of killing: physical contact, by sword or bat. We could say it fits the definition. But in order to be sure, we need to go further back, to see if he had killed others and to perform a personality check.[1]

According to Greek mythology, Theseus killed half a dozen people on his way to Athens where he was to meet his father Aegeus for the first time. And all of them had one characteristic in common: they were criminals. They were all murderers. Near Epidaurus,[2] he killed Periphetes who would rob travellers and kill them with his bronze club. These acts had earned him the nickname the Club-Bearer. Theseus killed Periphetes with his own weapon. Theseus' second victim was Sinis, whose nickname was the Pine-Bender because he would kill his victims in Corinth[3] by tearing them apart between two pine trees. Again Theseus would use the murderer's own modus operandi to execute him. His third victim was Sciron who forced people to wash his feet and then kicked them from a cliff into the sea, where they would be eaten by a giant turtle. Only this time it was the murderer who became the turtle's meal.

Later, in Elefsina,[4] Theseus killed Cercyon, who would murder travellers by his strong embrace while wrestling with them. Cercyon met the same fate at the hands of Theseus. Our hero's last victim before arriving to Athens was Procrustes. He

1. Joe Navarro, *Dangerous Personalities*, Rodale Books, 2014.
2. Epidaurus was an ancient Greece city, on the Argolis Peninsula in the Saronic Gulf.
3. Corinth was an ancient Greek city-state on the narrow stretch of land that joins the Peloponnese to the mainland of Greece.
4. Eleusis or Elefsina, an ancient Greek city in the Thriasian Plain, at the northernmost end of the Saronic Gulf.

would trick his victims, inviting them to rest in his home. He would force them into his iron bed, tie them up and either chop their legs or stretch their bodies to fit the bed's exact length. This bed turned out to be Procrustes' own deathbed.

Our profile is complete. We have a series of more than two victims. We have a certain type of victim: criminals. And the pattern is consistent: physical contact and, in five out of seven cases, Theseus employed the victim's modus operandi to kill them.

In regards to personality, Theseus' calm regard, his sculpted expressionless face with its coolness and absence of any hesitation, is consistent with a particular characteristic of serial killers: the lack of empathy and sentiments.

All in all, there is no doubt that Theseus could be classified as a serial killer. But in fairness, he killed people who were criminals themselves, the majority of whom were murderers. And because of these characteristics we could dub him "Antiquity's Dexter Morgan".

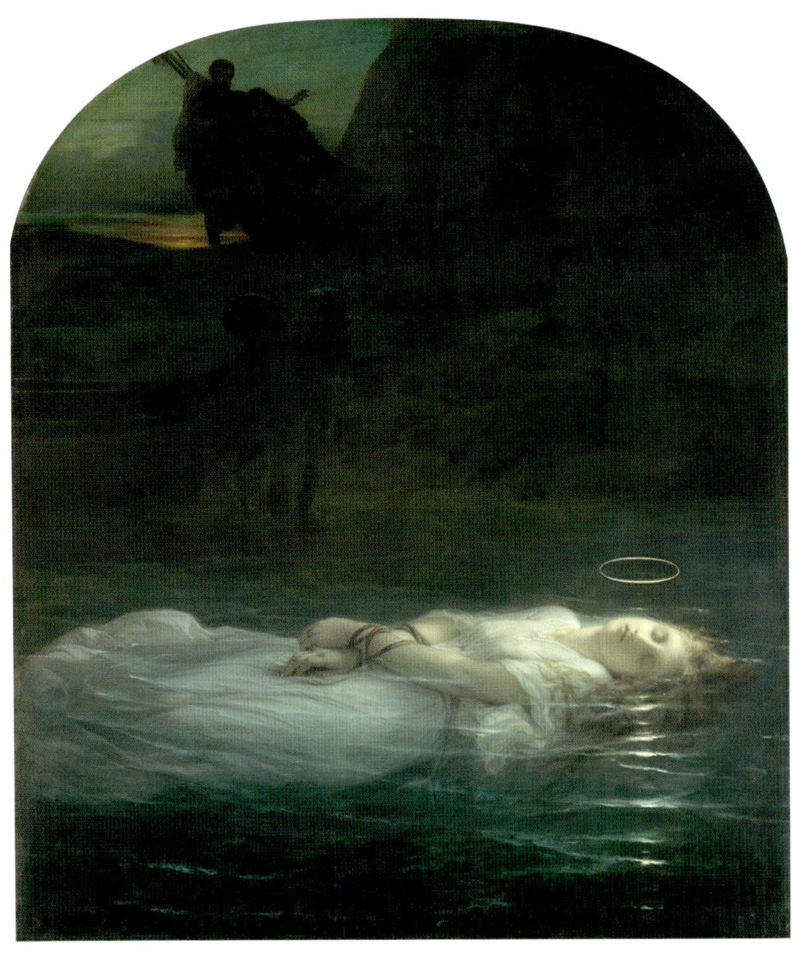

CHAPTER 26
YOUTH UNDER PERSECUTION

PERSECUTION

Paul Delaroche, *The Young Martyr*, 1855
H: 171 cm; L: 148 cm

First Floor, Denon, Salon Denon, Room 76

Persecution is the infliction of suffering or harm in an offensive way, by the government, upon those who differ in race, religion or political opinion.[1] Though this is the contemporary definition, the phenomenon itself – whether religious, political or ethnic – is as old as human civilization.

The scene we witness here is the result of such practice, during the 4th century AD. A young woman is floating on the Tiber River. Her white dress flows with the current, her hands are tightly bound. The darkness of the painting, the obscurity of the water and the nocturnal background are only illuminated by the dim light on her face, floating above the surface. Her watery grave will soon claim her entirely, erasing with it every sign of her beauty.

The halo above her pale face indicates that she is not an ordinary corpse. She is a martyr[2] as the title reads. In the background we can barely make out two figures, a man and a woman, possibly her parents. They are mourning, raising

1. James C. Hathaway, Michelle Foster, *The Law of Refugee Status*, Cambridge Univ. Press, 2014, p.186

2. A person who suffers persecution and/or death for advocating, renouncing, refusing to renounce, and/or refusing to advocate a belief usually of a religious nature.

their hands up to the sky and praying to the God she died for.

The year is 304 AD, a time of the most ruthless persecution of Christians in the Roman Empire, known as the Diocletianic or Great Persecution. With a series of Edicts,[1] starting in 303, the emperors Diocletian, Maximian, Galerius, and Constantius initially withdrew all legal rights from Christians and then ordered all inhabitants of the empire to offer a collective sacrifice to the Roman gods. Whoever did not abide by these Edicts, would be executed. More than 3,000 Christians were killed by burning, decapitation or drowning, and many more were tortured, until the issue of the Edict of Milan by the Emperor Constantine in 313 AD, which put a stop to the persecutions.

The young woman floating in the river is a victim of Diocletian's persecutions. She might have been tortured before being executed, but her beauty remains intact. Dressed in white, the colour of purity, she is the symbol of martyrdom.[2]

This painting would be Delaroche's last. The inspiration came to him in the form of a dream, while burning with fever. Yet in this work, "the saddest and most sacred of all his compositions" as he recounts,[3] we can sense, in an almost palpable way, the painter's personal grief. Death by ill health had taken Delaroche's beloved young wife at the age of thirty-one, in 1845.

1. A decree issued by a sovereign or other authority.
2. Exh. cat., *Paul Delaroche*, Paris: Musée du Louvre, 2012, p. 76.
3. Stephen Bann, *Paul Delaroche: History Painted*, Reaktion Books, 1997, p. 262.

Somehow death is even harder and more unjust when inflicted upon youth and beauty. Just before the young martyr is lost into the murky shadows of the river and before every light in the painting is extinguished, the allegory of the sacrificed youth is revealed.

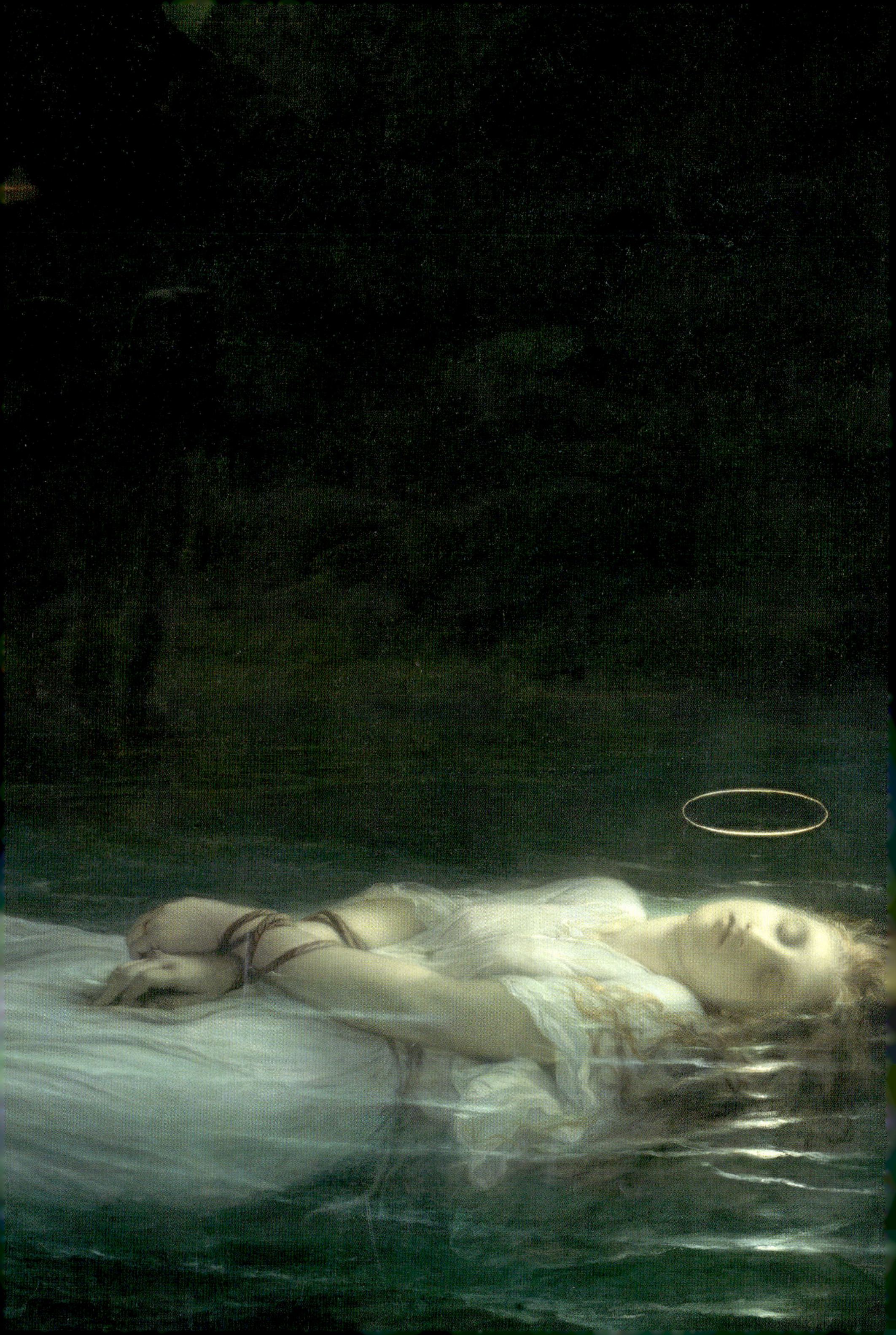

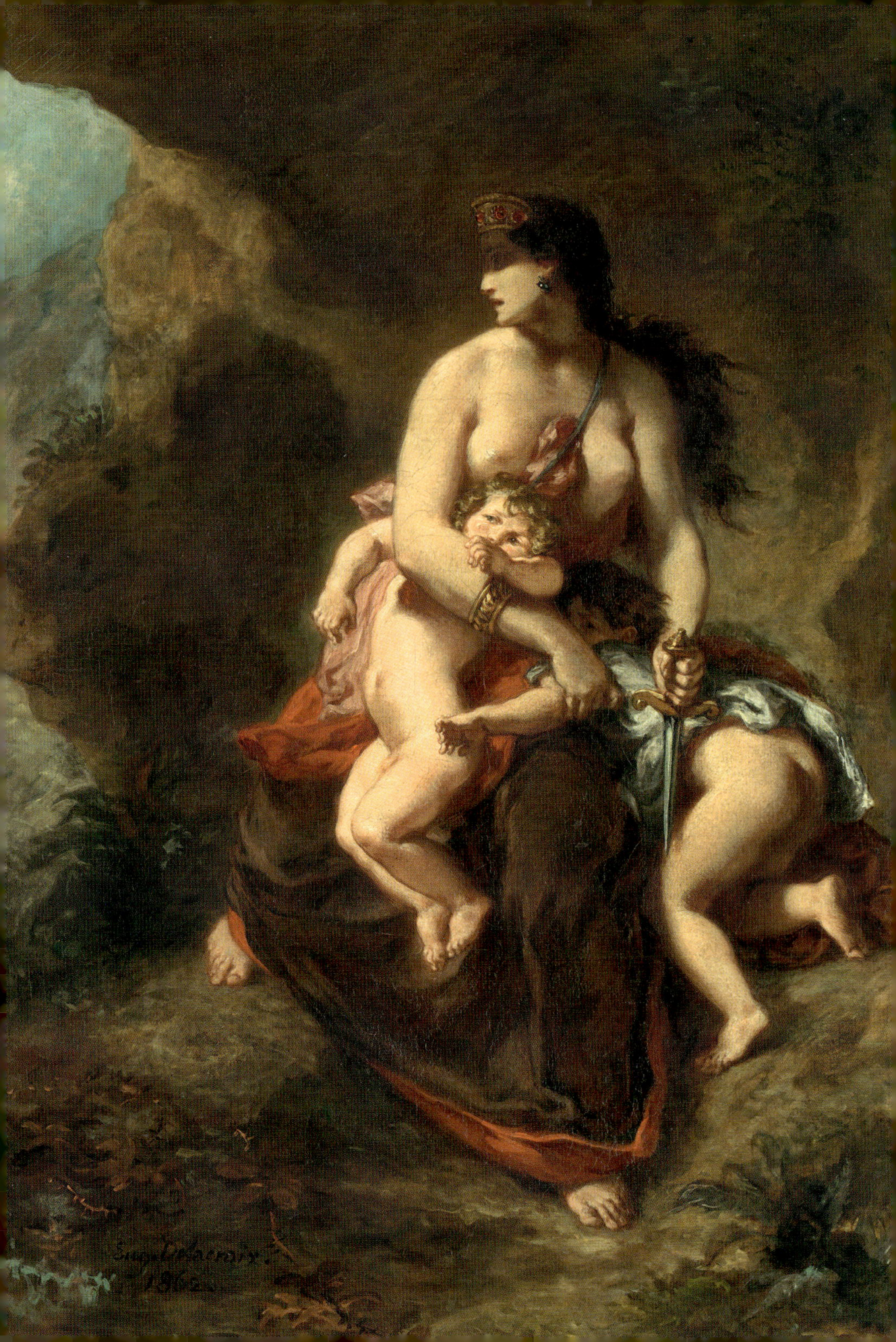
1862

CHAPTER 27
SEARCHING FOR THE TRUTH

INFANTICIDE - PEDICIDE - CRIMINOLOGICAL THEORY OF SOCIAL REACTION

Eugène Delacroix, *Furious Medea*, 1862
H: 122 cm; L: 84 cm

Second Floor, Sully, Eugène Delacroix, Room 62

When we look at this painting, which is a copy by Delacroix himself of his 1838 painting now in the Palais de Beaux Arts de Lille,[1] we can almost sense its violence. We see the movement of its protagonists, highlighted by the vivid colours, the dramatic play of light and shadow[2] and the panic of their postures. A woman enters a cave, her two children struggling frantically within her arms. But why would a child try to escape a mother's embrace? The knife in her hand might provide us an answer.

We are standing before Medea who, as per the painting's title, is in a mad, furious state. Dressed in the colours representing evil, red and black, her hands are closed in a tight grip: one around her sons and the other around a dagger. Her wild regard is fixed to her right, her black hair is dancing against the wind and her mouth is open like a beast, like a lioness, about to attack[3]. Whoever knows her story, knows her name is synonymous to infanticide or pedicide, the killing of a child by his own mother or father. The eyes of the brown-headed child

---

1. Eugène Delacroix, *Médée furieuse*, 1838, Oil on canvas, H: 260 cm; L: 165 cm, Palais des Beaux-Arts de Lille.
2. Jean-Louis Pinte, "Médée furieuse au Musée Delacroix, Une femme dans l'amour", *Figaroscope*, 5 May 2001.
3. In the original 1838 painting, her regard and her facial expression are much less threatening.

look at us, in bewilderment or pleading for help. The end of the blade almost touches his skin. He looks trapped between the naked breasts that fed him and the knife that could mark his death.

Medea is known as the sorceress, the barbarian, having committed fratricide (killing her brother) and infanticide. Yet Medea killing her own children is based on invention, upon a theatrical writer's idea designed to shock his public. Her story, in the original myth had a different ending, though not a happy one. So let's take it from the beginning.

Medea was a young and beautiful princess in Colchis,[1] daughter of King Aeetes and niece to the most powerful witch, Circe.[2] Circe was the one who taught Medea all about magic and potions. When the Argonauts arrived to her kingdom of Colchis, looking for the Golden Fleece, Medea fell in love with their leader, Jason. Forthwith, she decided she would help him steal the Fleece, thereby conspiring against her country and her own father. In exchange, she asked for only one thing: for Jason to marry her, take her away with him and love her forever. He promised he would, with the gods as his witnesses.

So Medea with her magic potions helped Jason perform the tasks that her father Aeetes had imposed upon him. Without her this would have been an impossible task, and Jason would have been killed from day one. So having successfully passed the tasks, Jason took the Golden Fleece and, along with Medea, fled Colchis.

---

1. A kingdom in the Southern Caucasus.
2. Circe was a sorceress, famous for turning Odysseus' crew into swine, according to Homer's *Odyssey*.

But Aeetes wouldn't let them get away so easily. He sent his ships to chase them down. To distract her father, Medea killed her brother, cut him into pieces and scattered his parts on the sea, so that the Colchidian ships would stop to collect them. Having betrayed her country and father and murdered her brother in the name of love, she expected this love to last forever. But it did not. Jason and Medea lived together for ten years in Corinth[1] and had five sons and a daughter. The two boys that we see in Delacroix's painting are Pheres and Mermeros.

Despite his oath, Jason fell in love with another woman: Glauce, the princess of Corinth. He announced to Medea that he was to marry the young woman, for the sake of their children who would, this way, rule over Corinth one day. Medea begged him to reconsider. She reminded him of his promise, made before the gods and of her help, without which he would never have obtained the Golden Fleece. She reminded him that she had betrayed all that was dear to her so she could be with him. But Jason ignored her pleas, and said it was Venus who had helped him, not her. Furthermore, it was he who had saved her by taking her away from her barbaric country and into civilized Greece. She was furious. As revenge, she sent a dress and a golden crown covered in poison to Jason's new bride. Soon, both Princess Glauce and her father, King Creon of Corinth, were dead.

Up to this point, the myth and collective knowledge of Medea's story is the same. But beyond this, the story we

1. Corinth was an ancient Greek city-state (polis) situated on the narrow stretch of land that joins the Peloponnese to the mainland of Greece.

know today was in fact created by the Greek tragic poet, Euripides, in 431 BC, with the objective of shocking the Athenian public. The truth was that the Corinthians, in an act of revenge for the death of their king and princess, killed Medea's children.

It was Euripides who had Medea kill her own children, sacrificing what she loved most, to avenge the man who betrayed her. And to the surprise of the Athenian spectators the holy city of Athens, their own city, welcomed and protected this woman, despite having killed her own sons.

This was a sign that her revenge was legitimate, as no one can break an oath given before the gods, as Jason did. This is why, even though Medea was a barbarian (which back then meant "not Greek"), Delacroix has her painted with the traditional Greek foot, with the second toe longer than the first. It might be an indication that Medea acted driven by honour and divine justice, as a Greek man would.

We therefore stand witnesses to this moment of ambiguity, between the two scenarios, the original myth and the myth as revised in Euripides' tragedy: "She advances toward the right, into a cave, turning backwards to make sure no one follows her. Her chest and arms are bare. She carries her two children and holds a dagger in her left hand."[1]

We will never know who she is looking at so fiercely, and therefore what the outcome of this painting is. Is it Jason approaching, and Medea about to kill their sons before his very eyes with her dagger? Or is it the Corinthians who will finally

1. *La Collection Thomy-Thiéry au Musée du Louvre. Catalogue descriptif et historique*, Paris: Librairie de l'art ancien et moderne, 1903.

take her boys from her arms and slay them, despite her vain attempt to protect her children with her knife?

As far as her standing is concerned, it would make no difference. According to the definition of the Criminological Theory of Social Reaction, if someone is perceived as a criminal within his environment, even if they are not, the social consequences would be the same as for a real criminal. This theory is applied here.

Even if Medea did not commit this crime, her name is and will forever be synonymous with harshness and extreme jealousy, in the public consciousness. She is, and will forever remain, the infanticide par excellence, the woman who committed the most unnatural of all crimes: killing her own children.

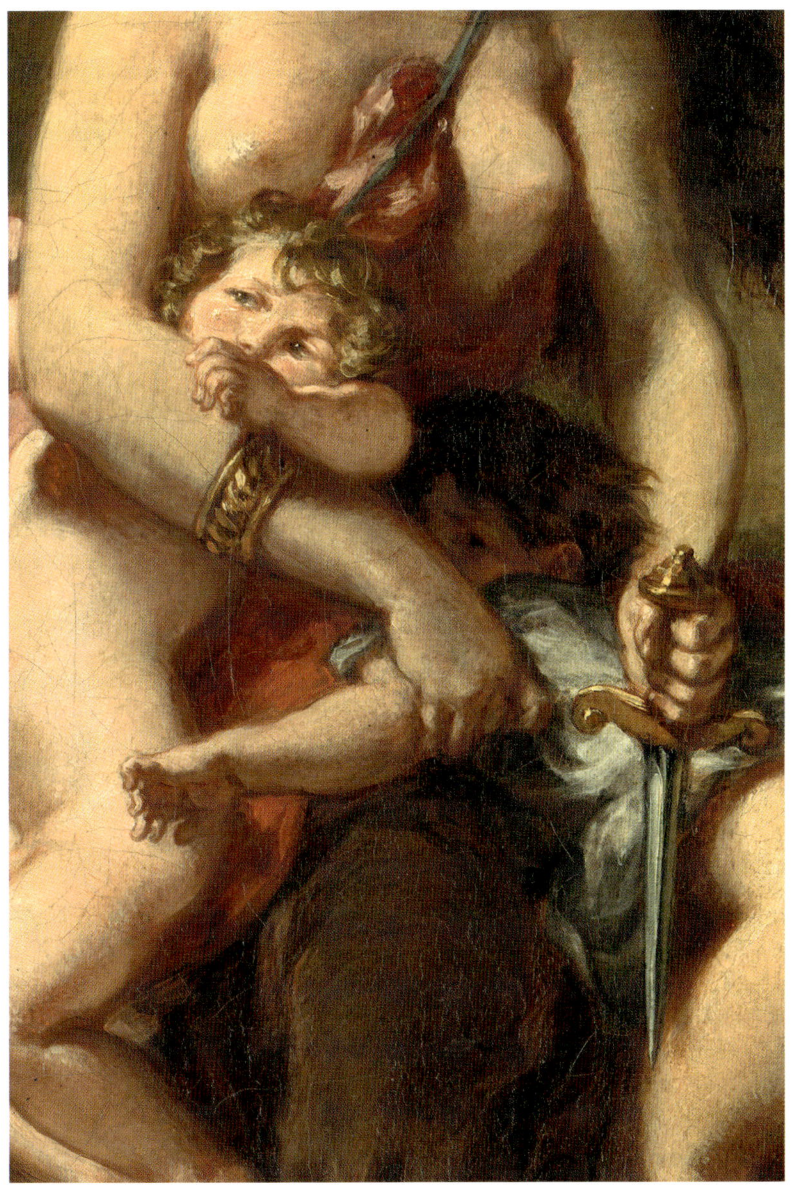

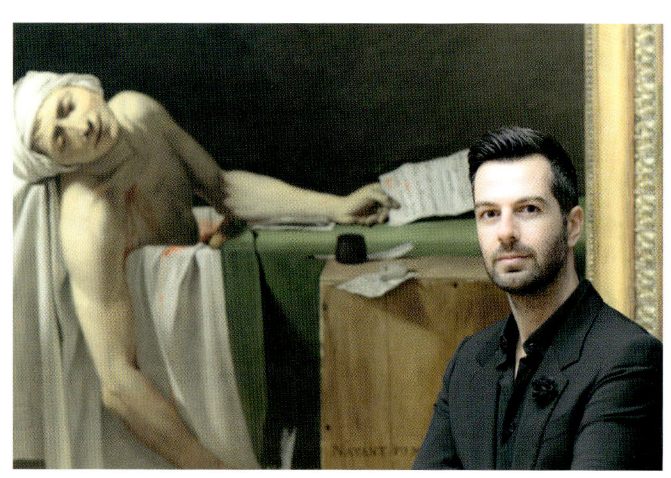

EPILOGUE

Our private criminartistic visit together is over. As your personal Virgil in this Dantenian tour of a murderous inferno, I guided you through truths and lies, secrets, vengeance, glory, pain and violent death – all in a place where ethics bow before aesthetics. At our every stop, perpetrators and victims set the scene, each one posing the same questions: Who did it? To whom? And why?

In contrast to an ever-evolving world, the protagonists you met here remain the same. They are, and forever will be, trapped in time, and unchanged within their frame or material. Their story is told, their act is committed, their fate is sealed.

It is you, my dear visitor, who has *changed* through this journey. You are no longer just a witness, nor a passive spectator. You have, in fact, become the detective who holds all the answers. You followed the clues, uncovered secrets, heard alibis and motives, learnt of untold truths. You have also taken on the role of a judge, composing and interpreting these truths, making up your mind, crafting your own conclusions and reaching your decision.

You are now equipped to sympathize or feel appalled by the killers' acts, afford them the benefit of the doubt, condemn or acquit them. It is now *your* call whether Medea is a monstrous mother or a misunderstood foreigner; whether Judith is a lustful killer or an obedient daughter; whether Herodes is guilty of killing a handful or thousands of children; whether Orestes is a born killer or not.

You have become the author of your own criminartistic truth.

ACKNOWLEDGMENTS

I would like to thank my Criminology Professors in Athens and Paris, especially Iakovos Farsedakis, Georgios Nikolopoulos, Antonios Maganas, Xavier Raufer and Alain Bauer for sharing their knowledge and their passion for this science.

I would especially like to thank my Thesis Director, Director of MA in Criminology at Panteion University of Athens, Christina Zarafonitou for her open mind, her help and support with my PhD research, a part of which has found its place in this book.

Many thanks to the enthusiastic team of Le Passage Editions, Marike Gauthier, Yann Briand, Barthelemy Chapelet and Vincent Eudeline for their wonderful collaboration, the fruit of which you hold in your hands.

My gratitude to Violaine Bouvet-Lanselle, who embraced this project from the beginning.

Special thanks to my friends and family, especially to Gianpaolo Nadalini, Niloufal Bakhtiar Bakhtiari and Clement Dureau-Hazera. They know why!

A big "Thank you" to Stephane Bern for his enthusiasm and faith in this project.

My gratitude – as always – to Prince Michael of Greece (Michel de Grèce) for his encouragement to dive into the deep waters of writing.

Last but not least, the biggest "Thank you" goes to Camille Delorean, without whose constant support, suggestions and late night exchanges on the manuscript, this book would have never seen the light of day!

SELECTIVE BIBLIOGRAPHY

Aggrawal, A., "Mass Murder" in Payne-James, J.J., Byard, R.W., Corey, T.S., and Henderson, C. (eds.) *Encyclopedia of Forensic and Legal Medicine*, vol.3 (London: Elsevier Academic Press, 2005).

Allard, Paul, *La Persécution de Dioclétien et le triomphe de l'église* (Paris: V. Lecoffre, 1890).

Allard, Sébastien, *Portraits Publics–Portraits privés, 1740-1830, Marat assassiné, La recherche de l'idéal* (Paris: RMN, 2007).

An Awful Warning or The Massacre of Saint Bartholomew, Inscribed to the memory of the late Rt. Hon Spencer Perceval (London, 1812).

Apsche, Jack, *Probing the Mind of a Serial Killer* (International Information Associates, 1993).

Auclair, Valérie, "L'œil médusé. Perspective et interprétations de Massacre du Triumvirat d'Antoine Caron (1566)", *Communications*, 85 (Paris: Seuil, 2009).

Avery, Charles, "From David d'Angers to Rodin – Britain's National Collection of French 19th-Century Sculpture", *The Connoisseur*, vol.CLXXIX (April 1972), p.234

Baldick, Robert, *The Duel: A History of Duelling* (London: Spring Books, 1970).

Bann, Stephen and Pacoud, Stéphane (eds.), *L'Invention du passé, Histoires de cœur et d'épée en Europe, 1802-1850* (Paris: Hazan, 2014).

Bann, Stephen, *Paul Delaroche, History Painted* (Reaktion Books, 1997).

Bartrop, Paul R., *Genocide: The Basics* (London: Routledge, 2015).

Becker, Howard S., *Outsiders: Studies in the Sociology of Deviance* (New York: Free Press. 1963).

Berger, John, *Ways of Seeing*, (London: British Broadcasting Corporation and Penguin Books Ltd, 1972).

Berger, Robert W., "Queen Thomyris with the head of Cyrus", *Bulletin of the Museum of Fine Arts Boston*, vol.77 (1979).

Berrebi, Éric-Henry, "Sardanapale ou l'impossible étreinte. L'écrit – voir. Figures de la mort", in *Revue d'Histoire des Arts*, no.8 (1986).

Bernheimer, Richard, "Theatrum Mundi", *The Art Bulletin* (Dec. 1956).

Black, Joel, *The Aesthetics of Murder* (The John Hopkins University Press, 1991).

Blanc, Charles, *Histoire des peintres de toutes les écoles, École française*, vol. 3, 1865, reprint of 1st edition (1862–63).

Bodres, Philippe, *Autour de Brutus de David: commentaires anciens et modernes* (Scenna Editions, 2001).

Bohrer, Frederick N., "Inventing Assyria: Exoticism and Reception in 19th century England and France", *The Art Bulletin*, LXXX (1988).

Bortnick, Barry, *Deadly Urges* (New York: Pinnacle, 1983).

Bowman, Franck Paul, "Le 'sacré-cœur' de Marat (1793)", Les fêtes de la Révolution, Colloque de Clermont-Ferrand, June 1974, *Sociétés des études Robespierristes* (Paris, 1977).

Brown, Mary, *Inside Art: Crime, Punishment and Creative Energies* (Winchester: Waterside Press, 2002).

Catherine Rosane, "La Mort de Sardanapale, ou le désespoir de Delacroix", *Profondeur de champs* (26 September 2012).

Chapman, Hugo, Exh. cat., *Michelangelo Drawings: Closer to the Master* (British Museum Press, 2005).

Chaudonneret, Marie-Claude, "Du genre anecdotique au genre historique. Une autre peinture d'histoire", in Exh. cat., *Les Années romantiques* (Nantes: Musée des Beaux-Arts, Paris: Galeries Nationales du Grand Palais, Plaisance: Palazzo Gotico 1995–96), p. 83.

Chaudonneret, Marie-Claude, *L'État et les artistes, de la Restauration à la Monarchie de Juillet (1815-1833)* (Paris: Flammarion, 1999).

Chefs-d'œuvre de l'art français, (Paris: Palais National des Arts, 1937).

Combes, Annie, *Agatha Christie, L'écriture du crime* (Paris: Les Impressions Nouvelles, 1989).

Constans, Claire, Beaulieu-sur-Mer: Conference, "Le théâtre grec antique: La tragédie, Actes", *Cahiers de la Villa Kerylos*, no. 8 (Paris, 1998).

Crow, Thomas, *Emulation. Making Artists for Revolutionary France*, (New Haven-London, 1995).

Cuin, Charles-Henry, *Durkheim: modernité d'un classique* (Paris: Hermann, 2001).

Culliver, Concetta C., *Female Criminality: The State of the Art* (Garland, New York: Garland Library of Sociology, vol. 22, 1993).

Cusson, Maurice, *Criminologie actuelle* (Paris: Les Presses Universitaires de France, Collection Sociologies, 1998).

Daskalothanassis, Nikos, Ο καλλιτέχνης ως ιστορικό υποκείμενο από τον 19ο στον 20ο αιώνα [The artist as a historical subject from the 19th to 20th century], Ekdosis Agra, 2004.

Davis, Carol Anne, *Women Who Kill* (London: Allison & Busby, 2002).

Delieuvin, Vincent, "Daniele de Volterra, Les deux faces d'un chef-d'œuvre," *Grande Galerie*, no. 17, (Sept.-Oct.-Nov. 2011).

Delieuvin, Vincent, "Quand la peinture s'attaque à la sculpture. Le combat de David et Goliath par Daniele de Volterra", *Grande Galerie*, no. 3 (March-April-May 2008).

De Quincey, Thomas, "On Murder Considered as One of the Fine Arts," *Blackwood's Magazine*, (1827).

Doğan, Recep, "Different Cultural Understandings of Honor That Inspire Killing", *Homicide Studies*, vol. 18, no. 4 (2015).

Douzinas, Kostas, Νόμος και Αισθητική, Λογοτεχνία Τέχνη, Δίκαιο [Law and Aesthetics, Literature, Art, Justice], Ekdosis Papazisis, 2005.

Durkheim, Émile, *Les Règles de la méthode sociologique* (1894) (Paris: P.U.F., 1960).

Eburne, Jonathan P., *Surrealism and the Art of Crime* (London: Cornell University Press, 2008).

Eddleston, John J., *Criminal Women, Famous London Cases*, True Crime series, (South Yorkshire: Wharncliffe Bookn, 2010).

Ehrmann, Jean, *Antoine Caron, Peintre de fêtes et des massacre* (Paris: Flammarion, 1986).

Eisner, Manuel, and Ghuneim, Lana, *Honor Killing Attitudes Amongst Adolescents in Amman, Jordan* (Wiley Periodicals, 2013).

Ellis, James, *Some reasons why "Capital punishment," or the sentence of death should be abolished, as proved by recent events: addressed to thoughtful readers* (London: E. W. Allen, 1879).

Enamels of Limoges: 1100–1350, Exh. cat., (Paris: Musée du Louvre, New York: Metropolitan Museum of Art, 1996), p. 168.

Farrington, David, and Murray, Joseph, *Labeling Theory: Empirical Tests* (New Brunswick, New Jersey: Transaction Publishers, 2014).

Farsedakis, Iakovos, and Sagounidou-Daskalaki, Iro, Στοιχεία εγκληματολογίας [Elements of Criminology], Nomiki Vivliothiki, 2007.

Ferri Enrico, *Les Criminels dans l'art et la literature* (Paris: Félix Alcan Editeur, 1908).

Fisher, Joseph, *Killer among us: public reactions to serial murder* (Westport, Conn: Praeger, 1997).

Forbes Winslow, Lyttleton, *The Insanity of Passion and Crime* (London, 1913).

Foucault, Michel, *Moi, Pierre Rivière, ayant égorgé ma mère, ma sœur et mon frère… : un cas de parricide au XIXe siècle* (Paris: Gallimard, 1973).

Fraser, Elisabeth A., "Delacroix's Sardanapalus: The Life and Death of the Royal Body", *French Historical Studies*, vol. 26, no. 2, (Spring 2003), published by Duke University Press.

Friedrichs, David O., *State Crime* (Aldershot: Ashgate, 1998).

Gaborit, Jean-René, ed., *Sculpture Française. II- Renaissance et temps modernes* (Paris: Editions de la RMN, 1998).

Galard, Jean, *Promenades au Louvre: En compagnie d'écrivains, d'artistes et de critiques d'art* (Paris: Robert Laffont, Bouquins, 2010).

Galitz K., Calley, "The Death of Virginia", in Exh. cat., *A Private Passion. 19th Century Paintings and drawings from the Grenville L. Winthrop Collection*, (Harvard University, 2003).

Gardner, Arthur R. L., *The Art of Crime* (London: P. Allan, 1931).

Gautier, Théophile, *Guide de l'amateur au Musée du Louvre* (1867) (Paris: Nabu Press, 2013).

Gill, Aisha K., Strange, Carolyn, and Roberts, Karl, *"Honour" Killing and Violence: Theory, Policy and Practice* (Basingstoke: Palgrave Macmillan, 2014).

Goodman, Derick, *Crime of Passion*, (London: Elek Books, 1958).

Graeme, Bruce Passion, *Murder and Mystery* (London: Hutchinson and Company Ltd., 1928).

Grayson, A.K. "The Chronology of the Reign of Ashurbanipal", *Zeitschrift fur Assyriologie*, 70 (1980).

Gregoriou, Christiana, *Language, Ideology and Identity in Serial Killer Narratives* (Routledge, 2011).

Grimal, Pierre, *Dictionnaire de la Mythologie grecque et romaine* (Paris, 1991).

Gruyer, F.-A., *Voyage autour du Salon Carré au Musée du Louvre* (Paris, 1891).

"Guérin. Une belle mise en scène", *Grande Galerie, le Journal du Louvre*, no. 15 (March–April–May 2011).

Guterman, Simeon L., *Religious Toleration and Persecution in Ancient Rome* (London: Aiglon Press, 1951).

Hanson, Helen, and O'Rawe, Catherine, *The Femme Fatale: Images, Histories, Contexts* (Basingstoke, UK: Palgrave Macmillan, 2010).

Hathaway, James C., and Foster, Michelle, *The Law of Refugee Status* (Cambridge Univ. Press, 2014).

Hatjinicolaou, Nicos, *Histoire de l'art et lutte de classes* (Paris: François Maspero, 1973).

Hautecœur, Louis, *Les Beaux-Arts en France. Passé et avenir* (Paris, 1948).

Hedgecock, Jennifer, *The Femme Fatale in Victorian Literature: The Danger and the Sexual Threat* Amherst (New York: Cambria Press, 2008).

Heide, Kathleen M., "Patricide and Steppatricide Victims and Offenders", *International Journal of Offender Therapy and Comparative Criminology*, vol.58, issue 11 (2014).

Helbronner, Evelyne, "Thésée combattant le Minotaure dit Thésée et le Minotaure, 1843", in *Catalogue raisonné des sculptures du XIXe siècle (1800-1914) des musées de Bordeaux*, PhD dissertation (Paris IV Sorbonne, 2003).

Herodotus, *The Histories*, translated by Sélincourt, Aubrey de (London: Penguin Classics, 2003).

Herum, Judith, *Byzantium, The Surprising Life of a Medieval Empire* (Penguin Books Ltd, 2007).

"Iconographie et problèmes de mise en scène: La mort d'Égisthe dans les 'Choéphores' d'Eschyle", *Revue Archéologique* (Presses Universitaires de France, 1978).

Ingrams, R.A., "Rubens and Persia", *The Burlington Magazine*, April 1974.

Jackson, Mark, *Infanticide: Historical Perspectives on Child Murder and Concealment, 1550-2000* (Aldershot: Ashgate, 2002).

Jacobs, Amber, *On Matricide: Myth, Psychoanalysis, and the Law of the Mother* (New York, Chichester: Columbia University Press, 2007).

James, P.D., *Talking About Detective Fiction* (Bodleian Library, 2009).

Jensen, Steven L.B., *Genocide: Cases, Comparisons and Contemporary Debates* (København: Danish Center for Holocaust and Genocide Studies, 2003).

Jensen, Vickie, *Women Criminals: An Encyclopedia of People and Issues* (Santa Barbara, Calif., 2012).

Jobert, Barthélemy, "Étude de tableau, Delacroix, La mort de Sardanapale", *Beaux Arts* (Dec. 1995).

Jones, Ann, *Women Who Kill* (New York: Holt, Rinehart & Winston, 1980).

Knepper, Paul, and Ystehede, P.J., *The Cesare Lombroso Handbook* (London: Routledge, 2013).

Kris, Ernst, and Kurz, Otto, *Legend, Myth and Magic in the Image of the Artist: A Historical Experiment* (New Haven and London: Yale University Press, 1979).

Kuper, Leo, *Genocide: Its Political Use in the Twentieth Century* (New Haven: Yale University Press, 1981).

L'École de Fontainebleau, Exh. cat. (Paris: Grand Palais, 1972).

L'Épée, Usages, mythes et symboles, Paris Musée du Cluny, Musée National du Moyen Âge (28 April–26 September 2011).

L'Épopée des rois thraces, Exh. cat. (Paris: Musée du Louvre, Somogy, 2015).

La Collection Thomy-Thiéry au Musée du Louvre. Catalogue descriptif et historique (Paris: Librairie de l'art ancien et moderne, 1903).

Lane, Brian, and Gregg, Wilfred, *The Encyclopedia of Mass Murder* (London: Headline, 1994).

Lavater, Johann Caspar (translated by Shaw, Samuel), *Physiognomy: or the corresponding analogy between the conformation of the features, and the ruling passions of the mind* (London: H. D. Symonds, 1800).

Laveissière, Sylvain, Exh. cat., *Prud'Hon, La Justice et la Vengeance divine poursuivant le Crime* (Paris: Éditions RMN, 1986).

Lester, David, *Serial Killers: The Insatiable Passion* (Philadelphia: Charles Press, 1995).

Libertés et contraintes, la peinture comme modèle pour la tragédie. Le Théâtre des Passions 1697-1759 (Musée des Beaux-Arts de Nantes, Éditions Fage, 2011).

Loire, Stéphane, "Adonis mort, un nouveau tableau de Laurent de la Hyre (1606–1656) au Musée du Louvre", *Études, Revue du Louvre*, 3 (1998).

Lombroso, Cesare, *L'uomo delinquente*, 1876.

Lombroso-Ferrero, Gina, *Criminal Man, According to the Classification of Cesare Lombroso* (New York: Putnam, 1911).

Louis XV. Un moment de perfection de l'art français, Exh. Cat., (Paris: Hôtel de la Monnaie, Nov. 1974–Mars 1975).

Lucian of Samosata, *True History* (Firestone Books, 2012).

Maeterlinck, Maurice, and Allinson, Alfred, *The Massacre of the Innocents* (London: G. Allen & Unwin, Ltd, 1914).

Maingon, Claire, *Le Salon et ses artistes. Histoire des expositions du Roi Soleil aux Arts Français* (Paris: Hermann Editions, 2009).

Malocco, David Elio, *Approaches in Criminal Profiling: An Introduction*, Student Guides Simplified series (CreateSpace Indpendent Publishing Platform, 2015).

Marrinan, Michael, *Romantic Paris, Histories of a Cultural Landscape, 1800-1850* (Stanford University Press, 2009).

Michel, Régis, *David contre David*, actes du colloque organisé au Musée du Louvre, 6–10 Dec. 1989 (Paris: Documentation Française, 1993).

Michel, Régis, *La Peinture comme crime ou la part maudite de la modernité* (Paris: Musée du Louvre, RMN, 2001).

Miquel, Pierre, *Les Guerres de religion* (Librairie Arthème Fayard, 1980).

Montaignon, Anatole de, and Guiffrey, Jules, *Correspondance des Directeurs de l'Académie de France à Rome avec les Surintendants des Bâtiments* (Paris, 1893).

Moret, Jean-Marc, "L'Ilioupersis dans la céramique italiote. Les mythes et leur expression figurée au IVe siècle", *Bibliotheca Helvetica Romana*, XIV (1975).

Morris, Edward, *The French Art in 19th Century Britain*, The Paul Mellon Centre for Studies in British Art (New Haven-London: Yale University Press, 2005).

Moscovici, Serge, *La Psychanalyse, son image et son public* (Presses Universitaires de France, 1961).

Navarro, Joe, *Dangerous Personalities* (Rodale Books, 2014).

Nikolopoulos, Giorgos, Όταν η εγκληματολογία συναντά τη λογοτεχνία: Ζητήματα διδασκαλίας και έρευνας [When Criminology meets Literature: teaching and research issues] in Tsouramanis, H – Kourakis, N – Zarafonitou, C, Εγκληματολογία: Διδασκαλία και έρευνα στην Ελλάδα [Criminology: teaching and research in Greece], Sakoulas, Athens – Komotini, 2011.

Noguères, Henri (translated by Engel, Claire Eliane), *The Massacre of Saint Bartholomew* (London: George Allen & Unwin, 1962).

Nourissier, François, and Foucart-Walter, Élisabeth, *Chiens* (Paris Musée du Louvre Éditions, Flammarion, 2007).

Oates, J. "Assyrian Chronology, 631–612 BC", *Iraq* 27 (1965).

Olson, Greta, *Criminals as Animals from Shakespeare to Lombroso* (Berlin/Boston: De Gruyter, 2013).

Paternoster, Ray and Bachman, Ronet, *Labeling Theory* (Oxfordbibliographies.com).

Patronos, Georgios, *The History of Jesus (from the manger to the empty tomb)* (Athens: Domos Editions, 1991).

Philippe Durey, "La Judith de François Ladatte", *La revue du Louvre et des Musées de France*, no. 3 (1982).

Piers, Maria W., *Infanticide: Past and Present* (New York: W. W. Norton & Company, 1978).

Pinte, Jean-Louis, "Médée furieuse au Musée Delacroix, Une femme dans l'amour", *Figaroscope* (5 May 2001).

Poletti, Michel and Richarme, Alain, *A.-L. Barye, Artiste et Artisan* (Paris: Univers du Bronze, Sculptures XIXe et XXe), p. 34.

Pomarède, Vincent, *Eugène Delacroix, La Mort de Sardanapale* (Paris: RMN, Service culturel Musée du Louvre, Collection Solo, 1998).

Pomarède, Vincent, and Grebe, Anja, *Le Louvre, toutes les Peintures* (Skira/Flammarion, 2012).

Pomarède, Vincent, and Trebosc, Delphine, *1001 peintures au Louvre: de l'antiquité au XIXe siècle* (Paris: Musée du Louvre, 2005).

Prat, Louis Antoine, Exh. cat., *Paul Delaroche* (Paris: Musée du Louvre, 2012).

Preez, Peter du, and Petrus, Wilhelmus, *Genocide: The Psychology of Mass Murder,* (London/New York: Boyars/Bowerdean, 1994).

"Quand Delacroix lisait Byron", *Beaux Arts magazine* (April 1996).

Rabate, Jean-Michel, *Given: 1° Art 2° Crime, Modernity, Murder and Mass Culture* (Brighton: Sussex Academic Press, 2007).

Raux, Sophie, "Carel Fabritius Eighteenth-Century Paris", *The Burlington Magazine*, no. 1307, vol. CLIV (February 2012), p. 104.

Roose, Max, *L'Œuvre de P. P. Rubens. Histoire et Description de ses tableaux et dessins*, vol. 4 (Anvers: Editions Jos. Maes, 1890).

Scailliérez, Cécile, *et al.*, "L'ardoise double face de Daniele de Volterra figurant David et Goliath. Étude et restauration d'une œuvre d'exception", *Technè*, no. 25 (2007).

Scailliérez, Cécile, "Salomé reçoit la tête de saint Jean Baptiste. La vengeance d'Hérodiade," (Louvre.edu, 1999).

Scott, John, *Social Theory: Central Issues in Sociology* (London: SAGE Publications Ltd, 2005).

Sérié, Pierre, *La Peinture d'histoire en France 1860-1900: La Lyre ou le poignard* (Paris: Arthena, 2014).

Sérullaz, Arlette, "Douze Dessins de Lethière au Louvre", *Études, La revue des Musées de France, Revue du Louvre* (1-2005), p. 78.

Shoham, Shlomo Giora, *Art, Crime and Madness* (Brighton: Sussex Academic Press, 2002).

Simkin, Stevie, *Cultural Constructions of the Femme Fatale: From Pandora's Box to Amanda Knox* (Hampshire: Houndmills, New York: Palgrave Macmillan, 2014).

Société des amis du Musée National Eugene Delacroix, "Études, À propos de la Médée Furieuse", *Bulletin*, no. 9 (Sept. 2011).

Soulié, Daniel, *Louvre secret et insolite* (Paris: Parigramme Éditions, 2011).

Spinelli, Margaret G., *Infanticide: Psychosocial and Legal Perspectives on Mothers Who Kill* (Washington: American Psychiatric Publishing Inc., 2003).

Suffert, Georges, "Simon Bertier, Clytemnestre, le retour en Grèce", *Le Figaro littéraire* (13 May 2004).

Summerfield, Giovanna, *Vendetta: Essays on Honor and Revenge* (Newcastle: Cambridge Scholars Publishing, 2010).

Thompson, Gregory, "Labeling in Interactional Practice: Applying Labeling Theory to Interactions and Interactional Analysis to Labeling", *Symbolic Interaction*, vol. 37, no. 4 (November, 2014).

Tibbetts, Stephen G., *Criminological Theory: The Essentials* (Los Angeles: SAGE, 2015).

Tiryakian, Edward A., *For Durkheim: Essays in Historical and Cultural Sociology*, (Aldershot: Ashgate, 2009).

Titus Livius (Livy). *History of Rome* (Ab Urbe Condita), English translation by. Rev. Canon Roberts (New York, New York: E. P. Dutton and Co., 1912), Book 3.44.

Vinson, R. J., "Émaux de Limoge", *Connaissance des arts*, no. 238 (December 1971), pp. 76–83.

Voïart, J.-P., *Entretiens sur la théorie de la peinture* (Paris: Alexis Eymery Libraire, 1820).

Wallace, Jonathan and Ellis Wild, Susan, *Webster's New World Law Dictionary* (Wiley Publishing Inc., 2006).

West's Encyclopedia of American Law, 2nd edition (The Gale Group, Inc., 2008).

Wilson, Colin, and Seaman, Donald, *The Serial Killers: A Study in the Psychology of Violence* (London: True Crime, 1992).

Wolff, Martha, *Northern European and Spanish Paintings before 1600 in the Art Institute of Chicago* (New Haven–London: Yale University Press, 2008).

Wright, Charles, *Constructions of deviance in sociological theory: the problem of commensurability* (Lanham: University Press of America, 1984).

Yardley, Elizabeth, and Wilson, David, *Female serial killers in social context: Criminological institutionalism and the case of Mary Ann Cotton* (Bristol: Policy Press, 2015).

Zarafonitou, Christina, Εμπειρική Εγκληματολογία [Empirical Criminology], Nomiki Vivliothiki, 2006.

Zorach, Rebecca, *Blood, Milk, Ink, Gold. Abundance and Excess in the French Renaissance* (Chicago: The University of Chicago Press, 2005).

PHOTOGRAPHIC CREDITS

© Photo Josse

for the entire photographs of this book with the exception of those mentioned in the following pages:

pages 86 and 91: © RMN-Grand Palais (musée du Louvre) / Tony Querrec
pages 92 and 97: © Christos Markogiannakis
page 118: © Musée d'arts de Nantes
page 119: public domain
page 176 (top): © RMN-Grand Palais / René-Gabriel Ojéda
page 176 (bottom): © RMN-Grand Palais (musée du Louvre) / All rights reserved
page 196: © Olivier Chevalier

printing of this work was completed on the presses of Pbtisk in Příbram

printed in Czech Republic

isbn : 978-2-84742-358-7

legal registration : April 2017